A Kaleidoscope of Models and Strategies for Teaching English to Speakers of Other Languages

A Kaleidoscope of Models and Strategies for Teaching English to Speakers of Other Languages

Deborah L. Norland, Ph.D.,
and Terry Pruett-Said

Teacher Ideas Press, an imprint of Libraries Unlimited
Westport, Connecticut • London

Library of Congress Cataloging-in-Publication Data

Norland, Deborah L.
  A kaleidoscope of models and strategies for teaching English to speakers of other languages /
by Deborah L. Norland and Terry Pruett-Said.
      p. cm.
  Includes bibliographical references and index.
  ISBN 1-59158-372-1 (pbk. : alk. paper)
  1. English language—Study and teaching—Foreign speakers. 2. Effective teaching. I. Pruett-Said,
Terry. II. Title.
PE1128.A2N64 2006
  428.0071—dc22   2006023739

British Library Cataloguing in Publication Data is available.

Library of Congress Catalog Card Number: 2006023739
ISBN: 1-59158-372-1

First published in 2006

Libraries Unlimited/Teacher Ideas Press, 88 Post Road West, Westport, CT 06881
A Member of the Greenwood Publishing Group, Inc.
www.lu.com

Printed in the United States of America

The paper used in this book complies with the
Permanent Paper Standard issued by the National
Information Standards Organization (Z39.48–1984).

10 9 8 7 6 5 4 3 2 1

Contents

Preface

This kaleidoscope is a collection of various ESOL (English to speakers of other languages) methods and models or orientations for those who teach or will teach English-language learners (ELLs). ESOL teachers may come in contact with these or wish to learn them for future reference. The methods and models are not just those that we, the authors, practice or recommend. In fact, we have tried to list as many strategies and models or orientations as possible in the hope that readers will be able to evaluate and discover which methods and models will work best for their particular teaching situations.

In an attempt to be as inclusive as possible, we have tried our best to cover the diverse realms of ESOL teaching. We have included methods and orientations that are practiced in K–12 schools, at the college and university level, and in adult education programs. A number of these methods and orientations may have different names in different situations, and we have tried to list the variations of these names. No doubt, however, there are terms for these methods and models that we have not encountered. In fact, there may be methods and models that we have not included, although we have tried our best to cover as much territory as possible. No methods, strategies, models, or orientations have been purposely left out. You may also notice that some of the methods/strategies and models/orientations may not be in current fashion. In an attempt to be inclusive we have incorporated these, but with comments regarding what we see as their inherent caveats.

Suggestions for Using the Text

The ESOL models and methods are listed in alphabetical order in the handbook. Variations on the orientations' and methods' names are listed next to the name we most commonly found attached to the method or orientation. We have then included a brief background on the method or model that includes when possible, a theoretical summarization of the method, its development, and its current use and application.

This is followed by the general strategy frequently used to teach and/or prepare curriculum using this method or model. In an attempt to make the strategy easily accessible we have presented the strategy in steps. Nevertheless, it is possible that in different situations certain steps might be eliminated or other steps added. In order to help readers conceptualize the method or orientation we have included some examples and applications. Again readers should be aware that these examples may not always be appropriate as is for their particular situation. But we would hope such examples would give readers the guidance needed to develop their own applications.

Although our goal is to present a resource of methods and models with objectivity and limited bias, we nevertheless feel it necessary to present caveats regarding the methods and models as we see them. In addition, we want readers to be aware that all methods and models may be inappropriate in certain situations, and thus, we have made comments in the "Weakness/Modifications" section regarding limitations of the methods and orientations as well as modifications that can be made in different situations.

In the process of accumulating these methods and orientations we have discovered that many of them overlap, and are definitely not entities in and of themselves. Thus, we have included a "See also" section that lists other methods which are compatible. At the end of each method and orientation we have included a list of materials in which readers may find more information regarding the method or model. Some of these materials give the theoretical and developmental background regarding the method or model. Others are collections of models for lessons and other applications. The lists are by no means exhaustive. The materials listed were chosen to give readers initial entry into the method or model presented.

Introduction

What Is ESL?

The acronym ESL stands for English as a second language. In the United States, ESL refers to the teaching of those students for whom English is not a first language. Some people don't like the term ESL, pointing out that in many cases English may be the third or fourth language of the students. In addition, in some countries, like India, Singapore, or Kenya, ESL has a slightly different meaning. In those places, it refers to the fact that English is a second official language that is learned in school and often used in government and business but may not be the first language of the majority of people.

In fact, a number of other terms are used to describe ESL. You may see the term ESOL (English for students of other languages). The acronym TESOL refers to "teaching English to students of other languages." TESOL is also the name of the professional international organization of teachers of ESOL. You may also see other terms such as ELL (English language learning) and ELD (English language development) used to describe students and programs that serve students who are learning English as a second language. You may also see the term LEP (limited English proficiency) to describe ESL students. However, most ESL practitioners dislike this term because they do not feel that ESL students are limited.

You may also see the term EFL, which stands for English as foreign language. Generally, EFL is used to describe English teaching that occurs in places where English is not the native language, and ESL is used to describe English teaching that occurs in places like the United States, Canada, England, and Australia where the first language of most people is English.

Who Are ESL Students?

In the United States, many different people are ESL students. Many are K–12 students, often immigrants who have recently arrived with their families. In other cases, they and their families may have been in the United States for a longer period of time. Many immigrant children, especially from refugee families, may have resided in a number of countries before arriving in the United States. Some of them may have limited schooling. Some of them may not know how to read and write in their native language. But other ESL students may have had very good schooling and may already be able to read and write in more than one language. Other students who may need ESL services are children adopted from overseas by American parents.

There are also native-born non-English students who may receive ESL services under the umbrella of bilingual education. These may include Native Americans, Pacific Islanders, and many Hispanics. Another group that sometimes receives language services under the umbrella of ESL are dialect-different students. These are students who speak a dialect of English different from the standard English used in a school or job setting in the United States. Many of these students may come from the Caribbean or countries such as Hong Kong and Malaysia where English is spoken but the dialect may be different enough to cause communication problems in the United States.

Many ESL students are adults. In some cases, they are international students who have come to the United States to study in higher education but need to improve their English skills before enrolling at a college or university. In other cases, they are already enrolled but need English support to help them improve their English. In other cases, adults immigrate to the United States. Like children, they have a wide range of education and language levels. Some adults may not be literate in their own language. In other cases, adults may have advanced degrees from their own countries and already know a number of other languages. Other adults come to the United States as visiting professionals in business or government. While here they may want to improve their English. Thus, the needs of ESL students can vary widely.

What's the Difference between an Approach, a Method, and a Technique?

In general an *approach* is viewed as an overall theory about learning language, which then lends itself to "approaching" language teaching and learning in a certain manner. A *method* is often viewed as a series of procedures or activities used to teach language in a certain way. A *technique* is usually seen as one activity or procedure used within a plan for teaching. The reality is, however, that language teaching professionals often find themselves in disagreement over these terms. Depending on how one is defining the term and the circumstances in which the term is being used, an approach may become a method or a method may become a technique. For this reason, we have decided to use *approaches* to describe all the ways of language teaching we present in our book. After our readers are introduced to these various approaches, they may decide for themselves how they wish to categorize them and how they fit into their syllabus.

So Which Approach Is Best?

There is no one best approach because the circumstances and needs of ESL students vary so greatly. To choose approaches that are the most appropriate for your students, you must take into account many variables. What are your students' needs? Where will they use their English? Will they need their English for school? Will they need their English for work? What kind of work do they do? How old are they? How much time do they have to learn English? Have they studied English or another language before? How well do they know their own language?

Which Approach Is Best for Certain Groups?

Even within certain groups there may not be one best approach. Nonetheless, there are certain approaches that tend to be used more often with certain groups than others. For example, in K–12 many ESL approaches are similar to the language arts approaches used to teach language to native speakers. We have grouped those approaches in the Language Arts section. But just as communicative approaches are also used with native speakers learning their own language, so they are frequently part of the teaching pedagogy of K–12 ESL teachers. It is also important to understand that students in school must learn the English used in school. This is especially important for ESL students who arrive in the United States at an older age such as middle school or high school. You will find some appropriate approaches for these students discussed under the Academic/Professional section.

In the United States, there are programs available for various types of adult ESL students. Many students who have just arrived may find themselves in adult basic education ESL programs sponsored by the government. These programs often use some of the approaches discussed in the Adult Literacy section. But such programs also make use of language arts approaches. In some cases, such as family literacy programs, both K–12 and adult basic education programs are involved in the same program. Other adult students are here as students in higher education or on a professional basis. Many of the approaches used for these students can be found in Chapter 5, "Academic and Professional Approaches."

Why Do We Need to Know about Various Methods and Approaches?

Although there may be no single best approach, there are best approaches for particular circumstances, as we mentioned earlier. In addition, to be a professional and an effective ESL teacher, one must be aware of the different theories and approaches that have developed. Most effective teachers choose from a number of approaches, methods, and techniques to create a learning environment that fits the needs of their students. They put these approaches together to create a varied syllabus and an optimum learning experience. Sometimes this is referred to as selective eclecticism. It may also be referred to as an organic or integrated syllabus or curriculum. This does not mean that teachers can just put together a bunch of activities to create a plan. Good teachers must always consider what the results of these activities will be and how these will form a long-term, effective program to teach another language.

Aren't Some Approaches Outdated?

Although it is true that some approaches become outdated as ESL practitioners find that they do not do a very good job of meeting either teachers' or students' needs, most have some strong points about them that tend to be borrowed to use with other approaches and thus have become a part of contemporary teaching approaches. In addition, there is a tendency in education for the popularity of approaches to swing back and forth. Thus, an approach that may be popular one decade may find itself out a favor in the next. This makes it all the more important that teachers be aware of the many approaches, with their strengths and weaknesses, so that they can use this knowledge to create an effective curriculum.

1

Historical Approaches

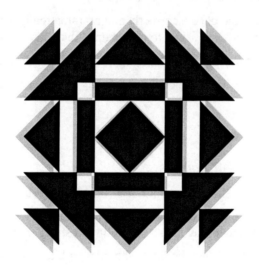

Audio-Lingual Method

English Skill Level: Beginning to Intermediate
Grade Level: Elementary to Adult (although older adults may find the quick recall difficult)

Background

The audio-lingual method (ALM) was developed during World War II in reaction to approaches that did not adequately develop speaking skills. ALM was strongly influenced by ideas from behavioral psychology that led to the belief that language was a system of habits that could be taught by reinforcing correct responses and punishing incorrect responses. In an ALM lesson, students are asked to repeat correctly the word or phrase that the teacher has said. Students are praised for correctly mimicking the teacher or are asked to repeat the phrase until it is correct. Although aspects of this method, such as drills in the beginning stages of language learning, continue to be used, most language educators now realize that language is more complex than mere mimicking.

Strategy

1. The teacher orally presents a phrase to the students.

2. Students are then asked to repeat the phrase quickly.

3. If a student pronounces the phrase correctly and grammatically, the student is praised. Students who do not say it correctly are asked to repeat until they can say it correctly.

4. The teacher modifies the phrase by changing a word in the phrase.

5. Students continue with drills in which they try to say the phrase quickly and accurately with various modifications.

Applications and Examples

Teaching Simple Present Tense

1. The teacher presents the simple present tense forms of a verb (or verbs) such as "like."

2. The teacher says, "I like, he likes (emphasizing the ending "s"), she likes, it likes, we like, you like, they like." The teacher may also add, "John likes, My mother likes," etc.

3. Students repeat chorally, "I like, he likes, she likes, it likes, we like, you like, they like."

4. The teacher then says the sentence "I like coffee." Then the teacher cues an individual student with the word "he." The student is expected to respond with "He likes coffee." If the response is incorrect, the student is corrected and asked to try again until he or she can say the sentence correctly. The teacher cues other students with other subjects, so that a replacement drill occurs rapidly around the room.

5. The teacher may then change not only the subject but also the object. For example, the teacher may say to a student, "He/tea." The student would correctly respond, "He likes tea." Then the teacher might give the cue, "They/parties."

6. The teacher might also use pictures instead of vocal cues. The teacher might then introduce the negative by modeling it, having students repeat it, and then do a drill in which students are cued (perhaps by an upturned or down-turned thumb) to make an affirmative or negative sentence.

Learning a Dialogue through ALM

1. The teacher presents a dialogue to the students. The teacher shows a picture of two people speaking to each other. Going through the dialogue, the teacher points to the picture to indicate who is speaking.

2. The teacher then repeats each line of the dialogue. The students repeat after the teacher.

3. The teacher repeats two lines of the dialogue as spoken by each person. One student is cued to say the first line of the dialogue. Another is cued to say the responding line. The teacher cues various students around the room to say the same thing. The teacher and students go through the dialogue in this manner until they have practiced all the lines of dialogue.

4. Then students are asked to perform the whole dialogue as a pair.

A Visual ALM Lesson

Presented by Becky Sutter, a Luther College education student

1. The teacher holds up a series of pictures of people with specific occupations. While showing each picture, the teacher says, "He is a firefighter" or "She is a police officer," etc. The students are instructed to repeat chorally the exact phrase that the teacher says right after she or he says it.

2. The teacher praises the students as a group for repeating the phrase correctly or will ask them to repeat it again if several students have trouble with it.

3. The teacher goes through the set of pictures again, this time calling on individual students and prompting them with the same prompts provided before. The teacher praises the students who repeat the phrase correctly and asks students who repeat it incorrectly to try again.

4. The teacher goes through the pictures a third time, this time changing the prompt. She or he calls on a student, prompts that person with a picture of an occupation, and says, "I," "you," "she," "we," or "they." The student is expected to produce a sentence such as, "They are cooks." The teacher either praises the student or asks the student to repeat the sentence after her (or him) depending on the accuracy of the response.

Strengths

- Controlled drills may encourage shy students to speak.
- Because ALM lessons and drills tend to go very quickly, they may help create a sense of fluency for some students.

Weaknesses

- Students who need the written word to reinforce their speaking and listening may find "pure" ALM very confusing.
- ALM frequently uses nonauthentic language.
- Some students may be unable to make the transition from controlled drills to more open-ended and creative language use.

Modifications

Although "pure" ALM insists on students learning listening and speaking before being exposed to the written word, in many cases, teachers may modify the method by writing information on the board or giving students the dialogues in written form.
See also: Direct Method

Further Reading

Chastain, K. (1971). *The development of modern language skills: Theory to practice.* Philadelphia: Center for Curriculum Development.

    This book provides a lot of background as well as examples of teaching practices using Audio-lingual and cognitive approaches.

Colvin, R. J. (1986). *I speak English: A tutor's guide to teaching conversational English* (3rd ed.). Syracuse, NY: Literacy Volunteers of America.

    Although not a book on ALM, this book presents a number of drills that was often used in ALM.

Larsen-Freeman, D. (2000). The audio-lingual method. In *Principles and techniques of language teaching* (2nd ed., pp. 35–51). Oxford, England: Oxford University Press.

    This resource is a presentation and analysis of an audio-lingual class.

Richards, J. C., & Rodgers, T. S. (2001). The audiolingual method. In *Approaches and methods in language teaching: A description and analysis* (pp. 50–69). Cambridge, England: Cambridge University Press.

    Richards and Rogers provide an overview of ALM including its theoretical and historical background and basic pedagogical procedures.

Direct Method

English Skill Level: Advanced Beginning to Advanced
Grade Level: Upper Elementary to Adult

Background

The basis of this method was developed in Europe by Francois Gouin in the 1880s. His premise was that it was best to learn another language by listening to it and speaking it just as children do instead of learning a set of grammar rules and vocabulary lists. The goal of this method is to teach students, usually adults, how to converse in everyday situations in another language. From this idea developed the direct method as an antithesis to the grammar-translation approach. A couple of decades later, the direct method was popularized in the United States by Charles Berlitz (who called it the Berlitz Method) and used it in his commercial Berlitz language schools. Other aspects of the direct method include classroom instruction exclusively in the target language, only everyday language is taught, and grammar being learned inductively. Although this method's initial insistence on using only the second language (L2) in the classroom as well as its lack of activities to develop reading and writing prevented it from being accepted in public education, it has, with modifications, influenced some contemporary approaches such as communicative language teaching, the natural approach, and total physical response.

Strategy

This method often develops around a set of pictures that portrays life in the country of the target language. From the beginning, students are taught, and must respond, in the target language. Besides pictures, realia and simple actions are used to get across meaning. Lessons often focus around question-and-answer dialogues. Correct pronunciation is also emphasized, but correct structure is not. Students may also read passages for information about the target culture. Teachers may ask questions about the reading to check comprehension, but it is never translated.

1. The teacher shows a set of pictures that often portray life in the country of the target language.
2. The teacher describes the picture in the target language.
3. The teacher asks questions in the target language about the picture.
4. Students answer the questions as best they can using the target language. Pronunciation is corrected, but grammatical structure is not.
5. Students may also read a passage in the target language.
6. The teacher asks questions in the target language about the reading.
7. Students answer questions as best they can using the target language.

Applications and Examples

1. The teachers shows a picture of a beach in Florida. (Tourist posters work well for this.)
2. The teacher describes the picture: "There is a beautiful beach in Miami. It is near the ocean. There are some people on the beach. They are wearing bathing suits. The woman is wearing a hat. The man is swimming. The children are building a sandcastle. There is a man selling ice cream. The children want to buy some ice cream. Their father will buy them some ice cream." The teacher may also use realia and other material to help students understand the vocabulary.

3. Students are asked questions such as:

> Where is the beach?
>
> What are the people wearing?
>
> What is the woman wearing?
>
> What is the man doing?
>
> What are the children doing?
>
> What is the man selling?
>
> What do the children want?
>
> Who will buy them ice cream?

4. Students give the answers. The teacher corrects pronunciation but is not overly concerned about grammatical correctness. The main goal is that students are communicative.

5. Students are then given a short reading about tourist attractions in Miami.

6. Students are then asked questions about the reading.

Strengths

- This is a quick way for students to learn basic conversation skills.

- This teaching method is helpful to teachers who do not know their students' first language (L1).

Weaknesses

- Some students may be overwhelmed without access to their first language.

- Higher-order discourse is not likely to be learned through this method.

- Not appropriate for learning academic literacy skills.

See also: Natural Approach, Communicative Language Learning

Further Reading

Bowen, J. D., Madsen, H., & Hilferty, A. (1985). Where we've been: insights from the past. In *TESOL: Techniques and procedures* (pp. 3–30). Boston: Heinle & Heinle.
> This text provides an informative summary of past language teaching approaches.

Celce-Murcia, M. (2001) Language teaching approaches: An overview. In *Teaching English as a second or foreign language* (3rd ed., pp. 1–11). Boston: Heinle & Heinle.
> This text provides an overview of past language teaching approaches with bulleted lists of their main points.

Larsen-Freeman, D. (2000). *Techniques and principles in language teaching* (2nd ed.). Oxford, England: Oxford University Press.
> This volume provides a discussion of the direct method including a sample lesson followed by an analysis of the principles of the method.

Grammar-based Approaches

English Skill Level: Advanced Beginning to Advanced
Grade Level: Upper Elementary to Adult

Background

Grammar-based approaches to language learning have been used since ancient times. The most well known of historical grammar-based approaches is the grammar-translation method in which students are presented a text and are asked to translate the text word for word. While translating, students' attention is brought to the appropriate grammar points to be taught. Although the grammar-translation method has fallen out of favor mainly because of its inability to foster communicative ability, other types of grammar-based approaches are still in common use. What most contemporary uses of grammar-based teaching have in common is the use of grammatical structures to guide the syllabus or lesson. Unlike earlier grammar-based approaches, more contemporary approaches, while presenting and using grammar points as a guiding force, enlarge on the grammar point to make the syllabus or lesson more communicative and authentic.

Strategy

1. The teacher presents the grammatical structure or rule.

2. Students practice of the structure.

3. Students use the structure in a holistic, authentic manner (in contemporary grammar-based approaches).

Applications and Examples

Teaching the Present Perfect Verb Tense

1. Students read a passage that makes use of the present perfect. Students are asked to recognize the present perfect. Students may also be asked why they think the present perfect is used in the reading.

2. The teacher then orally and visually explains the present perfect. One way to do this is to write the following on the board or overhead:

   a. How to make: subject + has/have + past participle

      Example: He   has   done   his homework over.
      Example: They   have   visited Chicago several times.

   b. When to use:

      For actions that began in the past and continue in the present.
      – I have lived in New York for five years.
      For repeated actions.
      – John has seen that movie five times.
      For an action that happened at an unspecified or unknown time.
      – She has already eaten lunch.

For an action that was just completed.
- Jane and George have just finished painting their house.

3. Students then do exercises to practice the tense. These exercises may be spoken or written exercises. Students may begin with exercises in which they only need to write in the correct form. Students may then do exercises practicing adverbs that often go with the present perfect such as *recently, until now,* and *so far.* In addition, they may practice exercises that ask them to recognize the difference between the simple present and the present perfect tense.

4. Students then do expansion and application exercises in which they practice writing or speaking about a topic that encourages them to make use of the present perfect. For example, students may write or speak about places they have visited or activities they have done since coming to the country they are in now.

Strengths

- Students who are analytical learners may need to know the grammar to make sense of a language.

- Students who have learned other languages through grammar-based approaches may find it easier to learn through this approach.

- Students, especially older ones, may need to know some grammar to reproduce the language correctly.

Weaknesses

- If grammar isn't taught as part of a whole, students may find that they know the grammar rules but not how to use the language. It must be emphasized to students that grammar is a tool to help learn a language, not a means to an end.

- Students may focus so much on grammar that they don't learn the other aspects of language.

- Students who are more holistic learners may find grammar lessons boring or even confusing.

Further Reading

Barbier, S. (1994). *Troublesome English: A teaching grammar for ESOL instructors.* Englewood Cliffs, NJ: Prentice-Hall Regents.
    This teacher-friendly reference and source book includes activities that can be used to teach students grammar.

Celce-Murcia, M. (1991). Grammar pedagogy in second and foreign language teaching. *TESOL Quarterly, 25,* 3.
    This informative article explains when grammar should be taught based on age, educational background, need, and goals of the learner.

Larsen-Freeman, D. (1997). *Grammar and its teaching: Challenging the myths.* Washington, DC: Eric Clearinghouse on Language and Literature. Retrieved May 3, 2006, from http://www.cal.org/resources/digest/Larsen01.html
    This brief article refutes ten popular language-learning myths about grammar learning and teaching.

Lock, G. (1996). *Functional English grammar: An introduction for second language learners.* Cambridge, England: Cambridge University Press.
    An in-depth presentation on the aspects of seeing grammar from a functional point of view as opposed to categorizing grammar formally.

Pennington, M. C. (Ed.). (1995). *New ways in teaching grammar.* Alexandra, VA: Teachers of Students of Other Languages (TESOL).

> This collection of activities and lessons is categorized by the grammar points that can be used to teach. It also includes an informative discussion of the situated process view of grammar learning and teaching.

Computer-Assisted Language Learning (CALL)

Grammar approaches lend themselves well to computer programs. A number of recent ESL grammar textbooks now have accompanying CDs and Web sites. Other grammar practice software include the following:

English on call, McGraw-Hill Contemporary.

> This three-level program uses contextualized, interactive activities to practice grammar.

ESL fitness, Merit Software.

> This beginner to low-intermediate program includes three levels that help students with English grammar, usage, and spelling.

ESL picture grammar, available from Audio-Forum.

> This interactive program helps students develop sentences and form verb tenses.

Focus on grammar CD-ROM, Longman.

> This four-level software program gives grammar practice through reading, listening, and writing activities.

Grammar 3D: Contextualized practice for learners of English, Heinle & Heinle.

> This four-level tutorial includes five hundred activities and thirty-four grammar topics.

The grammar cracker, Miller Educational Materials.

> This CD-ROM presents grammar rules and activities in an organized manner with work beginning with sentences and leading to essays and reports.

Let's go, Miller Educational Materials.

> Twelve CDs can be used to teach children language and grammar with dialogues, songs, vocabulary, phonics, and games.

Rosetta stone, Fairfield Technologies.

> This series focuses on listening exercises and is organized around grammar points.

Verbcon, Audio-Forum.

> This two-part program focuses on verb tense, aspects, moods, and voice.

2

Solo Approaches

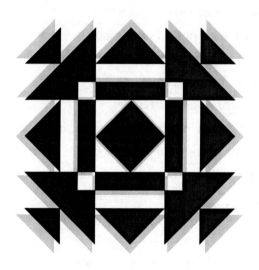

Community Language Learning

English Skill Level: Beginning to Intermediate
Grade Level: Elementary to Adult
Also Called: Counseling-Learning

Background

The psychologist Charles Curran developed community language learning (*Counseling-Learning in Second Languages*, 1976). Curran believed that students were often inhibited in learning a second language. In his method, teachers are viewed more as counselors and are expected to facilitate language learning as opposed to teaching it. He believed that creating a humanistic learning community would lower students' defenses and encourage open communication, thus allowing students to comprehend and absorb language more efficiently. This approach is an example of an affective approach. Affective approaches attempt to make students more emotionally comfortable within the classroom in the belief that if students are relaxed and open, they will be able to perform better.

Strategy

1.   Students sit in a small circle.

2.   The teacher stands behind a student.

3.   The student makes a statement or poses a question in his or her own language.

4.   The teacher translates the statement or question into the language being learned.

5.   The student repeats what the teacher said.

6.   The new phrase is recorded on a tape recorder.

7.   The procedure is repeated with other students until a short conversation is recorded.

8.   Students take a tape home or copy written conversation from the board to study at home.

9.   Direct instruction of grammar or vocabulary may take place from conversation.

Applications and Examples

Bedtime Routine

Submitted by Megan Larsen, Luther College education student

1.   The teacher reads the story *¿Es hora?* (M. Janovitz, North-South Books,1994) to the class. The class follows along with their own copies.

2.   The teacher brings the class together in a circle.

3.   The teacher chooses a student and stands behind him or her.

4.   The teacher starts the activity by asking, "¿Que es la primera cosa Lobito hacer en la cuenta?"

5.   The student makes a statement about the story in Spanish by answering the question. He or she may answer, "Lobito se da un chapuzon."

6.   The teacher repeats the statement the student made in English: "Si, Baby Wolf takes a bath."

7.   The student repeats the statement in English, "Baby Wolf takes a bath," while the teacher records it, either on audio or videocassette.

8.   The teacher moves on to the next student, who is asked to respond to the story.

9. After all the students have had a turn at speaking, the teacher and students listen to the tape together and make a list of new vocabulary the students learned—in both English and Spanish.

10. Students take home both the tape and the written vocabulary from the board.

Strengths

- CLL's humanistic approach, which views students and teachers as a community, and thus the teacher as more facilitator than teacher, fits in nicely with current trends in education.

Weaknesses

- CCL requires a number of conditions that may make it difficult to use in many situations. To be most effective, it requires teachers who are specifically trained in this method and also, ideally, trained in counseling techniques.

- CLL requires bilingual teachers and small, homogeneous classes.

Further Reading

Blair, R. W. (1991). Innovative approaches. In M. Celce-Murcia (Ed.), *Teaching English as a second or foreign language* (2nd ed.). Boston: Heinle & Heinle.
    A variety of techniques and approaches are presented in this text, including community language learning.

Larsen-Freeman, D. (2000). Community language learning. In *Techniques and principles in language teaching* (2nd ed., pp. 89–106). New York: Oxford University Press, 2000.
    An example of a community language learning lesson is presented and then analyzed.

Richards, J. C., & Rodgers, T. S. (2001). Community language learning. In *Approaches and methods in language teaching* (2nd ed., pp. 90–99). Cambridge, England: Cambridge University Press.
    Community language learning is among the models in this text examined for language teachers.

Stevick, E. W. (1998). *Working with teaching methods: What's at stake?* Boston: Heinle & Heinle.
    This is one of the volumes of the TeacherSource series. In this text, Stevick models a technique for teachers that enables them to be more self-reflective about the choices they make about the strategies and materials they choose to use.

Silent Way

English Skill Level: Beginning to Intermediate
Grade Level: Elementary to Adult

Background

The Silent Way, developed in the 1960s by Caleb Gattegno, is grounded in the belief that students should learn independently of the teacher. Gattengno proposed that students would learn better if they developed personal responsibility for their own learning. Thus, for much of the lesson, the teacher remains silent. Teaching is viewed as subordinate to learning. Students are encouraged to work with one another to figure out meaning. Students are introduced to new material once through the use of Cuisinare rods (small colored rods of varying lengths) and a series of wall charts. After the teacher introduces the material, it is up to the students to determine what they need to learn and independently work toward their academic goals. Certain aspects of this approach, such as the use of Cuisinare rods and developing student independence, continue to be used. However, this approach alone is rarely used because it is not practical within the classroom, and students need and desire more teacher input.

Strategy

1. The teacher introduces a discrete sound or structure by pointing at Silent Way charts or by using Cuisinare rods to demonstrate a structure or grammar point.

2. Students then figure out what they are learning and reproduce the sound or structure.

3. Between activities or sessions, students may ask questions of the teacher.

4. The teacher then introduces another discrete sound or structure in the same manner.

5. Students again figure out the meaning and reproduce the sound or structure.

6. As time goes on, students are ideally able to combine discrete sounds and structures to create longer strings of language.

Strengths

- Students are in an environment that encourages independence.

Weaknesses

- Some students may need more teacher input than what is provided through this method.

- Language is not learned as a whole nor is it authentic.

- Teachers must have access to materials and to the system.

Further Reading

Stevick, E. (1980). One way of teaching: The silent way. In *Teaching languages: A way and ways* (pp. 37–84). Boston: Heinle & Heinle.
> The silent way is only one of many strategies discussed for language teachers.

Richards, J. C., & Rodgers, T. S. (2001). The silent way. In *Approaches and methods in language teaching* (2nd ed., pp. 81–89). Cambridge, England: Cambridge University Press.
> A collection of strategies and techniques are included in this work for teachers of language.

Suggestopedia

English Skill Level: Beginning to Intermediate
Grade Level: Elementary to Adult (although adults who dislike background noise may find Suggestopedia frustrating)

Background

Suggestopedia was developed in the 1970s by Georgi Lozanov, a Bulgarian psychologist who contended that students have difficulty learning another language because of psychological barriers. He believed it is necessary to reach the students' unconscious for the new language to be successfully absorbed. If these barriers are removed, then students would be successful. To remove such barriers, Lozanov suggested drama, art, physical exercise, psychotherapy, and yoga. He also encouraged students to choose new names and identities. He especially believed that playing music in the background during a class, particularly Baroque music, created a relaxed state of mind in the students leading to the ability to absorb large quantities of information.

Strategy

1. Students sit in comfortable armchairs in a semicircle to create a relaxed atmosphere.

2. The teacher reads or speaks a new text in harmony with the music.

3. Students read the text that has been translated into the target language at the same time as the teacher says it in the native language.

4. There is a period of silence.

5. Next, the teacher repeats the text while the students listen but do not look at the text.

6. At the end, students silently leave the classroom.

7. Students are told to read the text quickly once before going to bed and once after getting up in the morning.

Strengths

- Some of the relaxation methods, including background music, may be helpful to students.

Weaknesses

- The method requires a class in which all the students share the same first language.
- It does not address speaking and writing.
- It is not communicative or creative.
- The majority of language acquisition researchers feel that Suggestopedia does not work.
- Few classrooms have comfortable armchairs.
- Some students may be bothered instead of relaxed by background music.

Further Reading

Richards, J. C., & Rodgers, T. S. (2001). Suggestopedia. In *Approaches and methods in language learning* (2nd ed., pp. 100–107). Cambridge, England: Cambridge University Press.
> Suggestopedia is examined in this collection of techniques for language learning.

Stevick, E. (1980). The work of Georgi Lozanov. In *Teaching language: A way and ways* (pp. 229–243). Boston: Heinle & Heinle.
> Suggestopedia is one of multiple strategies for teaching and learning language presented.

Stevick, E. (1980). Some Suggestopedic ideas in non-Suggestopedic methods. In *Teaching language: A way and ways* (pp. 244–259). Boston: Heinle & Heinle.
> Suggestopedia is one of numerous strategies for teaching and learning language presented.

3

Communicative Approaches

Communicative Language Learning

English Skill Level: Beginning to Advanced
Grade Level: Elementary to Adult

Background

Communicative language teaching (CLT) was developed in the 1960s from the research and writings of applied linguists in both Europe and North America who emphasized that language equaled communication (Canale & Swain, 1980; Savignon, 1983; van Ek, 1975). In Europe, this approach led initially to the institution of the notional-functional approach. In CLT, the goal of language teaching should not be translating and learning a set of rules but should be based on the goal of communicative competence. Communicative competence is most frequently defined as the ability to create meaning when interacting with others in the target language. Thus, the focus in CLT is on communication in authentic situations. Since the 1970s, this approach has been expanded on and has come to play a central role in most contemporary language teaching situations.

Strategy

Because CLT is such a broad orientation, it is difficult to give specific strategies. However, the broad guidelines are as follows:

1. Determine the communicative goals of the students.

2. Create situations and activities in which students produce authentic, meaningful, and contextualized communication.

3. Focus on accuracy only in as much as errors that would impede communication are corrected.

Applications and Examples

Authentic Role-Plays

In this lesson, students are introduced to a number of conversations that might occur when one is a visiting international student. Examples might include being invited to someone's house, making small talk at a party, being offered refreshments, and being asked to go out.

1. Students are asked what they would do and say in these various situations. This gives the teacher the chance to discuss not only vocabulary used but also cultural differences that might occur.

2. Students are given dialogues to practice in groups of two or three.

3. Students are encouraged to create their own variations on the dialogues.

4. Students are then given color-coded index cards that give them information about their role. For example:

    a. Blue card 1 says: You invite a friend over for pizza and beer.

    b. Blue card 2 says: A friend invites you over for pizza and beer. You want to come, but you don't drink alcohol.

    OR

    c. Pink card 1 says: You and a friend are at the mall shopping when you run into your roommate.

d. Pink card 2 says: Your friend introduces you to his or her roommate. You realize you've already met.

e. Pink card 3 says: You run into your roommate at the mall. The roommate introduces you to her or his friend.

5. Students with the same color cards come to the front of the room at the same time. Students are not allowed to see the other students' cards. The teacher tells the first person to start. Then the other students doing the role-play must respond spontaneously.

6. Other groups with the same color cards then participate in their role-plays.

7. By not allowing students to see each other's cards, the scene is set for a more spontaneous situation that is more authentic than if students practice set role-plays.

Presenting a Cultural Item to the Class

1. Students are asked what things or objects come to mind when they think of the country they are visiting. For example, if they are studying in the United States, they might say American football, rap music, hamburgers, or cowboy movies. The teacher writes these on the board as the students say them.

2. Students are asked to explain why they chose this particular object. Other students may also give their ideas on why this object represents the country they are visiting. Students may be asked if they agree or disagree.

3. Students are given the assignment for the next class period, when they are to bring in an object that represents an aspect of their culture. If they don't have the object, they may bring a picture or a mock-up.

4. Students show the object to their classmates. They explain what the object is, what it is used for or how it is used, and in what way it represents their culture. Other students are encouraged to ask questions.

Strengths

- Because the original impetus for this orientation was in reaction to grammar-based and audio-lingual approaches, the strength of CLT is that it creates a learning environment that closely replicates how students will use language in real-life situations. That is, students participate in real, authentic, and interactive language use in the classroom.

Weaknesses

- A caveat to this approach is that some practitioners may see communication as only oral/aural skills and may not put enough emphasis on the reading and writing skills that some students may need. Another caveat is that in an attempt to produce communicative skills quickly, accuracy may be overlooked or given little attention. Whether students will obtain that accuracy in time on their own continues to be an area of discussion in the ESOL field.

See also: Cooperative Language Learning; Experiential Language Teaching; Learner-Centered Approach; Notional-Functional Approach

Further Reading

Brumfit, C. J., & Johnson, K. (Eds.). (1979). *The communicative approach to language teaching.* Oxford, England: Oxford University Press.

> This volume compiles one of the first collections of articles advocating the communicative approach.

Canale, M., & Swain, M. (1980). Theoretical bases of communicative approaches to second language learning and testing. *Applied Linguistics, I*(1), 1–47.

Larimer, R. E., & Schleicher, L. (Eds.). (1999). *New ways in using authentic materials in the classroom.* Alexandra, VA: TESOL.

> This collection of lessons uses resources such as TV, radio, video, newspapers, magazines, academic and professional texts, and other authentic materials.

Lee, J. F., & VanPatten, B. (1995). *Making communicative language teaching happen.* New York: McGraw-Hill.

> This teacher training text discusses what is meant by communicative language teaching and proceeds to describe communicative language teaching in spoken language and reading and writing.

Savignon, S. J. (1983). *Communicative competence: Theory and classroom* practice. Reading, MA: Addison-Wesley.

> This was one of the first texts devoted to defining the need for the communicative approach in language teaching.

Savignon, S. J. (1997). *Communicative competence: Theory and classroom practice* (2nd ed.). New York: McGraw-Hill.

> Savignon is one of the initial proponents of communicative language teaching in the United States. This is the most recent edition of her discussion of communicative competence and communicative language teaching. She explores the theoretical and pedagogical background to the communicative approach, different approaches to syllabus design, various learning activities, and testing in the communicative classroom.

Savignon, S. J. (2001). Communicative language teaching for the twenty-first century. In M. Celce-Murcia (Ed.), *Teaching English as a second or foreign language* (3rd ed., pp. 13–28). Boston: Heinle & Heinle.

> In this chapter, Savignon provides an overview and discussion of the evolution of communicative language teaching.

Scarcella, R. C., Anderson, E. S., & Krashen, S. (Eds.). (1990). *Developing competence in a second language.* New York: Harper & Row.

> The editors compiled a collection of articles that explore communicative competence from a more theoretical language acquisition perspective.

Scarcella, R. C., & Oxford, R. L. (1992). *The tapestry of language learning; The individual in the communicative classroom.* Boston: Heinle & Heinle.

> This teacher training text uses communicative language teaching as its base.

Shameem, N., & Tickoo, M. (Eds.). (1999). *New ways in using communicative games in language teaching.* Alexandra, VA: TESOL.

> Using a collection of games, this text presents opportunities for students to be more communicative in the classroom.

Cooperative Language Learning

English Skill Level: All
Grade Level: All
Also Called: Collaborative Language Learning, Interactive Language Learning

Background

An interactive approach refers to language learning that is authentic and genuine and takes place between two or more people, and cooperative learning is the most frequent application of this approach. The goal of an interactive approach such as cooperative learning is to create meaningful learning experiences that will help students develop genuine fluency in another language. Cooperative learning consists of groups of students working together in a cooperative, as opposed to competitive, manner to complete a task, an activity, or a project. While working together, the students have meaningful interaction with one another in the target language. Both cooperative and collaborative learning refer to students working together in a group toward a goal, but collaborative groupings may also refer to teachers and students, parents and students, students and the community, or the school and the family collaborating.

Strategy

1. To implement cooperative learning, the teacher must decide whether cooperative activities will help meet the goals of the class. The teacher must also decide which type of cooperative activity to use. Cooperative activities might include peer tutoring, jigsaw activities in which different members of the group have different information that they must put together to find the results, group projects in which students work together to accomplish a task, and group projects in which students work independently but come together to complete the task. Then the teacher decides on one of many cooperative techniques to use, such as games, role-play, drama, projects, interviews, information gap activities, or opinion exchange.

2. The teacher decides how to put the groups together. Teachers might do this by counting off; by placing students in mixed-proficiency, similar-proficiency, or different or same language groups; or by allowing the students to choose their own partners. In general, the teacher should decide this ahead of time.

3. Once the teacher has decided on the cooperative activity, he or she explains to the group members what they will do. Sometimes each person in a group will be assigned a role such as recorder, leader, or negotiator. At times, it may also be necessary to model the technique and to explain why they will be working in groups. Then divide the class into groups.

4. Students begin, and the teacher checks with the groups to make sure that they understand what they are supposed to be doing. The teacher monitors the groups by walking around to make sure they stay on task if this is an in-class activity. He or she is also available to answer any questions or problems that may arise.

5. When the group is finished with its activity, which may take several minutes to several weeks depending on the activity, there should, in most cases, be a final product or discussion. Generally the final product, or parts of it, should be shared with the whole class. This might take the form of a formal presentation, a discussion, or a chance for everyone to ask questions.

From *A Kaleidoscope of Models and Strategies for Teaching English to Speakers of Other Languages* by Deborah L. Norland, Ph.D. and Terry Pruett-Said. Westport, CT: Libraries Unlimited/Teacher Ideas Press. Copyright © 2006.

Applications and Examples

Group Activity in an EAP Bridge Course

1. Students are organized into mixed-language groups. They ask each other preview questions that prepare them to begin a group study of an academic area such as psychology, sociology, marketing, language learning, or agriculture. For example, if the topic were language learning, students might be asked to discuss the following:

   a. What languages do you know?

   b. How did you learn those languages?

   c. Did you study them in school or learn them in some other way?

   d. What way do you think is best to learn a language?

   e. How old were you when you learned those languages?

   f. Do you think age makes a difference?

   g. What are some other variables that affect language learning?

   As a group, describe your conclusions about the best ways to learn another language.

2. After students are finished discussing the preview questions, the teacher asks each group to share its conclusions with the other groups.

3. Students are given an article to read about language learning. They are told to mark any areas of the article they find confusing.

4. After reading the article, students meet in groups to discuss both the content and the mechanics of the article. First, students compare the areas of the article that they found confusing or difficult and ask for help from other group members. The teacher then asks the groups members what they found difficult or confusing about the article and clarifies any information that may be giving them difficulties.

5. Students are given a set of questions or exercises to do as follow-up to the article. Students can either do the exercises independently and then compare answers, or they can work on the exercises together. The teacher can put answers to exercises on the board or an overhead, or the students and teacher can discuss follow-up questions.

6. Students are assigned to do a group speech on language learning. Students must research their speech by finding one journal article, doing an interview, and finding information on the Internet. Students are given in-class time to work on organizing their speeches.

7. Students give their group speeches. Each person in the group must give part of the speech, but it is up to the group to decide how the speech will be organized and who will be responsible for each part.

8. Other class members are also asked to make written comments on the group speeches. After all speeches have been given, groups write up their comments regarding the other speeches and turn this in to the teacher.

9. At the end of group work, students are asked to assess their groups as well as their contribution to the group.

10. The teacher gives a group grade for both the speeches and the group participation as well as individual grades based on each student's work and participation in the group.

Tall Tales

Submitted by Megan Larsen, Luther College education student

1. This lesson is based on the book *American Tall Tales* by M. P. Osborne (Alfred A. Knopf, 1991). Groups of students perform different tall tales for the class. The teacher enters the classroom dressed as a character from a tale from *American Tall Tales* and tells that tall tale to the class.

2. The students are placed in groups of four or five. They can choose their groups by picking a numbered card; all students with the same number combine to form a group.

3. Each group chooses a tall tale and reports to the teacher which they have chosen. The teacher provides a copy of that particular story to the group.

4. The groups read their stories aloud among themselves. Each group member will take a turn reading.

5. The members of the group make a list of the various characters in their tale. They then decide who will play each role and place that person's name next to the character's. The characters do not necessarily have to be people; a group member could play a tornado or Babe the Blue Ox. This list should be turned in to the teacher.

6. The groups rehearse acting out their tale. Students use their own words to act out the tale, although they can use language similar to that in the book. The teacher walks around the classroom helping groups and checking their progress.

7. After students have had a chance to rehearse, each group performs its tale for the class.

8. After each group has performed its tale, students write a journal entry on the various tall tales that were performed, as well as the specific tall tale their group performed. Students write about how they felt about working with their group to complete the final presentation and about what his or her personal role in the group. It can also include information that they have learned about tall tales so far.

Strengths

- When students are interacting in groups, they are required to use authentic and fairly fluent communications skills, which prepare them for the actual communication skills they will need in real life.

Weaknesses

- For group work to be successful, it must be carefully planned. A weakness in this method is that some teachers may just put students in groups without planning and find that the groups are not particularly successful. Some students may resist cooperative work if they do not understand the purpose.

Further Reading

Brown, H. D. (1994). *Teaching by principles: An interactive approach to language pedagogy.* Upper Saddle, NJ: Prentice Hall.

    This book presents an overview of when teachers should use or avoid group work and how to implement group work successfully in the classroom.

Enright, D. S. (1991). *Teaching English as a second or foreign language.* Boston: Heinle & Heinle.

This general article on supporting English language learners in the classroom includes sections on collaboration grouping and developing a sense of community in the classroom. (A later edition of the book does not include this section.)

Johnson, D. M. (1994). *Educating second language children: The whole child, the whole curriculum, the whole community.* Cambridge, England: Cambridge University Press.

Johnson maintains that it is not enough to focus on only language learning in the English language classroom. Educators also need to review and consider the collaborative roles of family, school, and community.

Kessler, C. (1992). *Cooperative language learning: A teacher's resource book.* Englewood Cliffs, NJ: Prentice Hall.

This collection of articles covers a wide range of issues with lots of teaching examples. A particularly strong section on cooperative methods in mainstream subject areas will help ESL and multicultural students succeed.

Nunan, D. (1992). *Collaborative language learning and teaching.* Cambridge, England: Cambridge University Press.

The chapters in this text represent a variety of issues pertaining to collaborative learning and teaching, including experimental language learning, literacy considerations for English language learners, how to build collaborative language learning environments, cooperative learning, and team teaching and curriculum development.

Prapphal, K. (1993). *Methods that work: Ideas for literacy and language teachers* (2nd ed.). Boston: Heinle & Heinle.

Rivers, W. (1987). *Interactive language teaching.* Cambridge, England: Cambridge University Press.

TESOL Journal (1999, Summer). *Collaborative classrooms: Where competence, confidence, and creativity converge, 8*(2).

This special issue is devoted to collaborative language teaching with articles on collaborative writing, building cultural community, and do's and don'ts of collaborative learning.

Experiential Language Teaching

English Skill Level: Advanced Beginning to Advanced
Grade Level: Elementary to Adult
Also Called: Task-based Teaching, Project-based Teaching

Background

Experiential language teaching (ELT) initially grew out of educational and psychological theories proposing that a subject is learned best if students are involved in concrete, hands-on experiences with the subject. The American educator John Dewey was one advocate of the method. The belief is that students will learn better if they use the language as opposed to being passive receptors of artificial language. It is also thought that students will be able to analyze and discover their own information about the topic and language use as they are involved with tasks or projects. In language teaching, ELT creates situations in which students *use* their new language instead of just learning about it. This method is seen as particularly well suited for use with children but is now being practiced with students of all ages in many learning situations.

Strategy

ELT's main strategy is to have students be involved in doing. An experiential language lesson can be conducted in multiple ways, and a number of different activities can be included under the umbrella of ELT. For example, realia, show-and-tell, games, and videos are examples of teacher-fronted ELT activities. Because the focus of ELT is more often on the student than on the teacher, however, student-centered activities such as hands-on projects, cross-cultural experiences, field trips, role-plays, and simulations are frequently used ELT activities. In addition, poetry, songs, and drama may also be considered ELT activities.

1. The teacher identifies a task or activity that will help students learn the language needed in their particular context.

2. The teacher plans how the task should be implemented including any necessary language items that may need to be introduced or reviewed for the students to perform the task or activity.

3. The teacher explains the task to the students.

4. The students discuss the task and identify their roles.

5. The students do their task or activity.

6. The students perform or demonstrate what they have learned or accomplished.

Examples and Applications

If a student needs to know how to do a job interview in English, the following activities might be executed:

1. The student does an exercise in which he or she is asked to comprehend questions with question words such as *what, where, how, who, when,* and so on.

2. The student listens to examples of job interviews.

3. The student and teacher analyze the grammar, vocabulary, and discourse of the interviews.

4. The teacher or the students (or both together) create the dialogue for their own interview.

5. The students practice and then role-play interviews.

Strength

• Students are involved in actually using the language in authentic situations.

Weaknesses and Modifications

• Experiential activities must be carefully thought out with their goals and pedagogical purposes kept in mind or experiential activities may end up having little or no educational value.

See also: Cooperative Language Learning; Whole Language

Further Reading

Bygate, M., Skehan, P., & Swain, M. (Eds.). (2001). *Researching pedagogic tasks: Second language learning, teaching and testing.* Harlow, England: Longman
   This collection of research-based articles explores the foundations of tasks for language learning including their use in the classroom and testing.

Eyring, J. L. (2001). Experiential and negotiated language learning. In M. Celce-Murcia (Ed.), *Teaching English as a second or foreign language* (pp. 333–344). Boston: Heinle & Heinle.
   The authors begin the article by summarizing the history of experiential learning and conclude with lots of information about various projects and guidelines on how to organize project work.

Moss, D., & Van Duzer, C. (1998). *Project-based learning for adult English language learners.* National Center for ESL Literacy Education. Retrieved November 17, 2005, from http://www.cal.org/caela/esl_resources/digests/ProjBase.html
   This online article online presents an overview of project-based learning.

Nunan, D. (1989). *Designing tasks for the communicative classroom.* Cambridge, England: Cambridge University Press.
   Nunan's seminal book on designing tasks covers the design and implementation of tasks in the classroom. It also includes an appendix of tested examples.

Rodrigues, R. J., & White, R. H. (1993). From role play to the real world. In J. W. Oller (Ed.), *Methods that work: Ideas for literacy and language teachers* (2nd ed.). Boston: Heinle & Heinle.
   This is an early collection of practical strategies for teaching reading, writing, listening, and speaking.

Willis, D., & Willis, J. (2001). Task-based language learning. In R. Carter & D. Nunan (Eds.), *The Cambridge guide to teaching English to speakers of other languages* (pp. 173–179). Cambridge, England: Cambridge University Press
   The text attempts to connect language theory and research into practical classroom applications.

Willis, J. (1996). *A framework for task-based learning.* Essex, England: Addison Wesley Longman.
   Willis's teacher-friendly text guides teachers through the process of setting up task-based learning in their classrooms.

Notional-Functional Approach

English Skill Level: Advanced Beginning to Advanced
Grade Level: Elementary to Adult

Background

The Council of Europe developed this approach in the 1970s to serve as a paradigm for language teaching in Europe. In this model, the content of what should be taught focuses on notions and functions as opposed to a grammar-based curriculum. Notions are content areas such shopping, health, travel, personal identification, and so on. Functions are how we use language such as expressing opinions, asking for advice, apologizing, and so on. Concepts presented in this approach have been subsumed by experiential language teaching.

Strategy

The following format is often used:

1. A dialogue focusing on certain functions and notions is presented.

2. Students practice the dialogue with classmates.

3. Students may create their own dialogues for role-playing.

4. Students may reinforce usage through assignments in which they choose or fill in the appropriate words in a written dialogue.

5. Students may expand on the previous tasks by going into the community and practicing "real-life" dialogues.

Strengths

- Pragmatic, authentic use of language is emphasized.

- The approach helps students to understand different registers of language.

Weaknesses

- The approach can be too limited with little focus on academic or professional needs and skills.

Further Reading

Finocchiaro, M., & Brumfit, C. (1983). *The functional-notational approach.* New York: Oxford University Press.
   A presentation of the functional-notational approach with an emphasis on learning language in real-life situations.

Total Physical Response (TPR)

English Skill Level: Beginning to Intermediate
Grade Level: Elementary to Adult (although method may need to be modified for secondary and adult English language learners)

Background

James Asher developed total physical response, frequently called TPR, in the 1960s and 1970s. He believed that learning new vocabulary in conjunction with corresponding motor activity would reinforce the learning of words and expressions—especially in children, but he also advocated its use with adults. Active participation also keeps students interested. Asher also believed that the use of such commands would reduce anxiety levels and make use of the right brain.

Strategy

1. The teacher gives commands such as

Open the door	Touch your nose	Draw a circle
Close the window	Stand up, sit down	Draw a square

2. The student completes the action of the command.

3. If the student does the command correctly, the teacher knows the student understands the command.

4. The student's understanding is reinforced by performing the action.

Applications and Examples

Classroom Commands

1. The teacher gives the following command to all the students: "Open your book."

2. Students open their books.

3. The teacher gives another command such as, "Put your pencil on your desk."

4. Students put their pencils on their desks.

5. The teacher gives another command such as, "Raise your hands."

6. The teacher continues to give commands related to classroom actions. The teacher may model the actions if students have not attempted such commands or actions before. The teacher may also give commands to individual students such as, "Erase the board."

7. Students may also give commands or instructions to each other.

TPR Storytelling

In storytelling, TPR is used to introduce a story to students.

1. The teacher should select a story with plenty of action.

2. The teacher uses TPR commands to teach vocabulary used in the story. Students can also act out commands. Students can be put in pairs to give and act out commands.

3. The teacher presents a mini-story (often part of a longer story) that students learn and retell or even revise. More mini-stories are presented and practiced.

4. The teacher presents the whole story. Students then retell the story. Students may also do various exercises related to the story such as true-false, open-ended questions, writing about the characters, and so on.

5. Students create their own stories. Students may write and illustrate their stories, use drama to act them out, or videotape their stories.

Strengths

- Results in lower anxiety levels among language learners.
- An activity or movement reinforces language learning in authentic ways.

Weaknesses and Modifications

- In its original form, TPR may be too limited to use alone. Thus, TPR is often used at the beginning levels or as part of a more complex lesson. It is also possible that commands can be lengthened into a process. For example, the teacher can say, "draw a square with a line through it. Then draw a triangle on the right side of the square," and so on. Teachers can have students use problem-solving tasks such as showing three boxes with different pictures inside and say, "touch the box where the woman is standing."

- Other modifications include having students take a more participatory role by giving commands or instructions to one another. TPR can also be done in a game form such as "Simon Says." Advocates of TPR have also developed the method into TPR Storytelling.

Further Reading

Asher, J. (2000). *Learning another language through actions* (6th ed.). Los Gatos, CA: Sky Oaks Productions.

    This volume outlines classroom applications of the TPR approach.

Marsh, V. (2000). *Total physical response storytelling: A communicative approach to language learning.* Retrieved April 26, 2006, from http://www.tprstorytelling.com/story.htm

    This site includes information, lessons, and materials on TPR storytelling, a strategy that combines the use of stories with TPR actions.

Nelson, G., & Winters, T. (1993). *Operations in English: 55 natural and logical sequences for language acquisition.* Brattleboro, VT: Pro Lingua Associates.

    Exercises in this book can be used in the classroom to facilitate learning of English for students who speak it as a second language. Tasks in which students give instructions on how to do various operations such as using a calculator, mailing a letter, or making a paper airplane are presented.

Richard-Amato, P. A. (1996). The total physical response and the audio-motor unit. In *Making it happen: Interaction in the second language classroom* (pp. 115–126). White Plains NY: Longman.

    Richard-Amato's chapter examines total physical response with examples of commands; the role of the audio-motor unit of commands inclusive of the natural language approach; the application of jazz chants, music, and poetry; storytelling, drama, and games; and affective activities.

Seely, C., & Romijn, E. K. (1995). *TPR is more than commands—at all levels.* Los Gatos, CA: Sky Oaks Productions.

    Seely and Romijn's resource explains how teachers can use TPR to move students from zero English language proficiency to fluency in English. The TPR commands are complex and include dialogues, role-playing, and storytelling.

4

Language Arts Approaches

Language Experience Approach

English Skill Level: Beginning to Intermediate
Grade Level: Primary (Lower Elementary) to Adult

Background

Originally developed to teach reading and writing to preliterate monolingual students, this approach was later used to teach literacy skills to adults, including those learning English as an additional language. Supporters of the language experience approach (LEA) believe that students can learn to read and write by using their own level of oral vocabulary. In addition, because students are using subject matter familiar to them, the information will be relevant to their needs.

Strategy

1. The student tells a story, usually based on a real-life experience, to the teacher.
2. The teacher writes down the story exactly as it is told including the errors made.
3. The student reads the written story with the teacher helping as needed.
4. After the student is comfortable reading the story, individual words, grammar points, and so on may be studied.

Strengths

- Schema is already present so students have immediate understanding of text.
- Students can see that the symbols of reading have personal and authentic meaning.
- Students are learning literacy skills at their own level.

Weaknesses

- Because it requires some knowledge of oral L2 vocabulary, it may not work with adults or older children with limited speaking skills or who are afraid to speak in the target language.
- Some believe this approach may reinforce errors if there is not enough adequate follow-up.

Modifications

- Stories may be done as a group with students giving sentences that the teacher writes on the board. Students may take turns giving sentences to create a narration. Editing can also be done as a group.
- Teachers may decide to write the story (or some aspects of it) correctly at the same time as the student shares the story.
- Students can be put in multilevel groups to write stories so that those with more writing skills can help those just learning.
- Students can write plays or act out stories.

Further Reading

Hawkins, B. (1991). Teaching children to read in a second language. In M. Celce-Murcia (Ed.), *Teaching English as a second or foreign language*. Boston: Heinle & Heinle.
    This methodology resource provides theory and practical applications for the classroom.

Richard-Amato, P. A. (1996). *Making it happen: Interaction in the second language classroom—from theory to practice*. New York: Longman
    Richard-Amato's sourcebook examines theory, classroom methods, activities, and practical concerns about classroom management and organization.

Taylor, M. T. (1993). *The language experience approach and adult learners*. Retrieved May 4, 2006, from the National Center for ESL Literacy Education Web site: http://www.cal.org/caela/esl_resources/digests/LEA.html
    This is an overview of the language experience approach with implementation ideas for the classroom.

Literature-based Approach

English Skill Level: Advanced Beginning to Advanced
Grade Level: Elementary to Adult

Background

Instead of teaching reading through traditional, bottom-up approaches using basal readers, students are given the opportunity to explore reading through the use of authentic texts. There are various methods within the parameters of this approach, including literature-based discussion groups outlined here.

Strategy

1. Students use authentic literature to explore various genres including realistic fiction, fantasy, historical fiction, biography, and so on.

2. Students work in cooperative groups for shared reading and are expected to complete various tasks individually, such as notating unfamiliar vocabulary, making predictions, participating in group discussions, and so on.

3. Students within the group are assigned various tasks or roles, such as discussion leader, group recorder (audio and written), word wizard, geography locator, and research specialist.

4. Students work together to determine various literary elements in the story—characters, plot, setting, and so on.

5. The teacher checks the accuracy of students' interpretations through group or individual dialogue.

6. Students are encouraged to make meaning by discussing various issues in the text with relevance to their lives.

7. A multitude of breakout activities can be incorporated after reading the text.

8. Assessment can be authentic or traditional.

Applications and Examples

1. Students divide into groups. After the teacher presents booktalks for several books, students select the one they want to read. Students can use the "five-finger" strategy to determine whether a book is the appropriate reading level. Also, when initially starting literature groups, it is helpful to start with one book for the entire class to work through the process together. (*Number the Stars* by Lois Lowry is one example.)

2. Within the group, various roles are assigned.

3. Students can choose to read the book aloud or silently, meeting after reading a specified portion. The teacher can assign this, or with more autonomous groups, the students can set the pace.

4. The teacher wanders from group to group, listening to discussions, providing input as needed, and perhaps inquiring to ensure accuracy in comprehension.

5. After reading the book, students select from a multitude of activities to extend the text. Students can choose to work individually, in pairs, in a group, or on multiple projects, if time allows. The teacher initially provides help, but students can make suggestions of their own.

6. When students complete their projects, they share them with the class and perhaps the rest of the school community.

Strengths

- English language learners encounter authentic literary texts. This means that students read books and stories written as literature rather than specially written stories designed with controlled vocabulary to develop particular reading skills.

- Students may develop a love of reading. They feel a sense of empowerment and become voracious readers.

- Books are read in English.

Weaknesses

- Effective only with intermediate and advanced students.

- Vocabulary can be potentially overwhelming if English language learners do not have appropriate strategies to use. Texts include words used in new ways, used colloquially, used with specific cultural referents, or used metaphorically. Teachers need to teach strategies such as inferencing to help learners.

- Literature reflects cultural values, shared knowledge, and discourse organization, which may be different from that of students' native cultures.

- "Speed readers" finish the books ahead of the rest. Others may be slower readers.

Further Reading

Fidere, A. (1999). *Practical assessments for literature-based reading classrooms.* New York: Scholastic.

   Fidere's reading instruction has students engaging in experiences with authentic texts and raises a significant concern about assessment. This book provides multiple strategies for assessing students in a literature-based reading program to provide teachers with an accurate picture of the students' skill and plan future instruction.

Fitzsimmons, P. (2002). *Kick starting the inner site: Reading to see and feel.* Brisbane, Australia: Annual Meeting for the Australian Association for Research in Education. ERIC Document Reproduction Service No. ED478114

   This article explores the emotional and academic impact that reading aloud and discussing authentic literature in the classroom can have on students. It also gives examples of how to work toward a literature-based reading program.

Natural Approach

English Skill Level: Advanced Beginning to Intermediate
Grade Level: Elementary to Adult
Method: Natural Approach

Background

An approach or method developed in the 1970s by Stephen Krashen and Tracy Terrell emphasizing that people "acquire" languages best by learning naturally like children do. Krashen and Terrell believed that comprehension should precede production and that students should not be forced to speak until they are ready. They proposed that production would emerge in stages. They believed that the course syllabus should be based on communicative goals and that activities should be planned to lower the affective filter and eliminate, as much as possible, any anxiety that students may feel about speaking a new language. In theory, if these principles are followed, students will feel comfortable with the new language and learn the language at an automatic level just as children learn their first language (L1). The approach is intended to help students acquire, as opposed to learn, a new language so that they will be able to understand and speak it automatically and fluently.

Strategy

1. The teacher speaks to the students in the target language at a level they can more or less understand. The teacher may use pictures, actions, or realia to communicate meaning.

2. The teacher asks questions that the students can answer. As students become more comfortable with the language, more difficult tasks such as role-plays, open-ended dialogues, discussion, and group work can be used.

3. Students do not have to speak until they are ready to. They can be encouraged to speak but should not be forced to do so. The focus should be on communication, and error correction should be limited and nonthreatening.

Strengths

- Students are more likely to participate actively and meaningfully when they feel they are ready to do so.

- Students can become fluent in the target language.

- Such an approach lowers the anxiety level of students, which is not only kinder but also more likely to produce positive results.

Weaknesses

- The approach does not address academic needs of students, including reading and writing.

- Some students may need more impetus to speak.

- Students, especially older learners, do not necessarily learn a second language (L2) as they learned their first language (L1).

Modifications

- When warranted, teachers may need to translate the directions into the student's first language (L1). This changes the approach, however, and assumes the teacher is fluent in the student's first language.

Further Reading

Krashen, S. (1995). What is intermediate natural approach? In P. Hashinpur, R. Maldonado, & M. VanNaerson (Eds.), *Studies in language learning and Spanish linguistics in honor of Tracy D. Terrell* (pp. 92–105). New York: McGraw-Hill.

    This collection of scholarly articles focuses on language teaching methodology.

Krashen, S., & Terrell, T. (1983). *The natural approach*: *Language acquisition in the classroom.* Englewood Cliffs, NJ: Prentice Hall.

    This text presents an overview of the natural approach, a method for students that are in the beginning stages of learning social language skills in a second language

Richard-Amato, P. A. (1996). The natural approach: How it is evolving. In P. A. Richard-Amato *Making it happen; Interaction in the second language classroom* (pp. 127–154). White Plains, NY: Addison-Wesley.

    This is a sourcebook for language teachers that explores theory, classroom methods and activities, and practical concerns about classroom management and organization.

Terrell, T. (1991). The role of grammar instruction in a communicative approach. *The Modern Language Journal, 75*(1), 52–63.

    Suggestions on ways explicit grammar instruction may be useful in an acquisition-based communicative approach.

Whole Language Approach

English Skill Level: All
Grade Level: All

Background

Whole language philosophies or approaches focus on the use of authentic language that is meaningful to students, proceeding from whole to part and integrating development of language modes and domains. This approach is a constructivist philosophy of learning that places emphasis on the integration of language and content, fostering personally and academically meaningful language development. Listening, speaking, reading, and writing—the four language modes or skills—are taught as an integrated whole, with written and oral language developed simultaneously. Whole language focuses on using language, focusing on meaning first, getting students to write early and often, accepting invented spelling for beginners but expecting conventional spelling as students advance in the writing process, exposing students to high-quality literature and authentic texts from diverse written genres, allowing students to make choices in reading, and encouraging all to be voracious readers. Lessons are learner centered and meaningful to students' lives inside and outside of school. Language lessons engage students in social interaction and collaborative learning. The focus is on the social construction of meaning and understanding through the process of reading and writing. Students first acquire literacy through their own writings and share children's literature as well as experiences across the curriculum through science experiments, recipes, games, instructions for making things, math problem solving, interactive computer communications, and map reading. Language is developed for meaningful purposes inside and outside of school. Whole language avoids the practices of teaching skills in isolation (sounds, letters, grammar rules, and words) or in a strict sequence, using books with controlled vocabulary, or using worksheets and drills.

Strategy

1. This approach immerses students in a rich language and literacy environment.

2. The teacher provides time, materials, space, and activities for students to be listeners, speakers, readers, and writers.

3. The teacher focuses on the whole because the mind makes sense of or constructs meaning from experiences—whether the experiences are spoken, listened to, read, or described in writing—when they are communicated as wholes.

4. The teacher acts as a communication role model in listening, speaking, reading, and writing so that instruction, function, and purpose are meaningful.

5. The teacher creates an atmosphere of expectancy and a climate that is encouraging and supportive in which students are expected to continue their literacy development and feel comfortable doing so.

Applications and Examples

1. To make the story *The Little Red Hen* more relevant to students' lives, the teacher could ask students about times when they've needed help but no one was willing to give them aid, or a discussion could be shared about bread—eating it, baking it, favorite kinds, and so on.

2. The teacher reads aloud from the big book *The Little Red Hen,* written in the native language to lay the foundation for initial comprehension in a bilingual classroom. If in a classroom with diverse native languages, this step is omitted.

3. The teacher reads aloud the English big book version of *The Little Red Hen*. While reading, the teacher models predicting, demonstrates by pointing left-to-right directional reading, looks at pictures for clues, uses voice projection during dialogue, and so on.

4. In subsequent readings, the students read (choral reading) the main dialogue sections, "Not I, said the (animal)?" and the teacher may use cloze techniques (i.e., stopping to have students fill in words). As a cloze exercise, transform the passage "Once there were four friends—a pig, a duck, a cat, and a little red hen," to "Once there were _____ friends—a pig, a _____, a cat, and a little red." Children complete the blanks using the pictures in the story as clues.

5. After choral reading, the teacher asks the students to retell the story and writes on sentence strips. The teacher may teach students about using dialogue (quotation marks) to indicate speaking.

6. Students use the sentence strips to put the story into the correct sequence.

7. The students make animal masks and role-play the story.

8. Students are allowed to check out student copies of *The Little Red Hen* to read at home for pleasure.

9. Students could create their own copies of the book or perhaps expand the original by adding more animals to the story.

10. Extension activity: Students could make bread or pretzels in class.

Pretzels

(from http://bread.allrecipes.com/az/BrdPrtzls.asp)

Ingredients

   1 1/2 teaspoons active dry yeast

   3/4 cup warm water (110 degrees F/45 degrees C)

   1/2 teaspoon white sugar

   1/4 teaspoon salt

   2 cups bread flour

   1 egg, beaten

   2 tablespoons kosher salt

Directions

1. In a small bowl, dissolve yeast in warm water. Let stand until creamy, about 10 minutes.

2. In a large bowl, combine yeast mixture, sugar, salt, and 1 cup flour; beat well. Beat in the remaining flour, 1/2 cup at a time, until a stiff dough is formed. Place dough in a lightly oiled bowl, cover, and let rise until doubled in volume.

3. Preheat oven to 450 degrees F (230 degrees C). Lightly grease a cookie sheet.

4. Turn dough out onto a lightly floured surface and divide into 12 pieces. Roll pieces out into long sticks and form into pretzel shape. Place pretzels on prepared baking sheet. Brush with beaten egg and sprinkle with kosher salt.

5. Bake in preheated oven for 12 to 15 minutes, until golden brown.

Strengths

- Whole language allows interactions with a variety of texts, experiences, and activities in a classroom atmosphere that supports literacy development.

Weaknesses

- Performance can be difficult to evaluate objectively when using authentic assessment.

Further Reading

Barton, B. (Reteller). (1993). *The Little Red Hen big book.* New York: HarperTrophy.
   This is a Big Book edition of the classic fairy tale *The Little Red Hen.*

Freeman, Y. S., & Freeman, D. E. (1998). *ESL/EFL teaching: Principles for success.* Portsmouth, NH: Heinemann.
   Freeman and Freeman provide a discussion of teaching English as a second language/ English as a foreign language, including descriptions of exemplary teaching methods and ideas.

Froese, V. (Ed.). (1996). *Whole language practice and theory* (2nd ed.). Boston: Allyn & Bacon.
   A text that guides teachers through structuring, planning, and delivering instruction using a whole language program.

Harp, B. (Ed.). (1991). *Assessment and evaluation in whole language programs.* Norwood, MA: Christopher-Gordon.
   Harp offers techniques and ideas to guide student assessment and evaluation in whole language programs.

Raines, S. C. (Ed.). (1995). *Whole language across the curriculum: Grades 1, 2, and 3.* New York: Teachers College Press; Newark, DE: International Reading Association.
   This book from the Language and Literacy Series published by the International Reading Association helps teachers design and implement curriculum using the whole language philosophy.

Whitmore, K. F., & Crowell, C. G. (1994). *Inventing a classroom: Life in a bilingual, whole language learning community.* York, ME: Stenhouse.
   Activities, including Drop Everything and Read (DEAR), link theory and practice in this resource that presents the foundations of a whole language philosophy within the context of a bilingual learning environment.

5

Academic and Professional Approaches

Cognitive Academic Language Learning Approach

English Skill Level: Advanced Beginning to Advanced
Grade Level: Elementary to Adult

Background

This approach was developed by Anna Chamot and J. Michael O'Malley to help secondary-level students make a successful transition into their regular high school classes. The cognitive academic language learning approach (CALLA) is a three-pronged approach focusing equally on academic language learning, academic content learning, and learning strategy instruction. Lessons built around academic content include various exercises that focus on language skills, study skills, and content-specific concepts. Chamot and O'Malley encourage the use of the following instructional methods and concepts in their approach: language across the curriculum, language experience approach (LEA), whole language, process writing, cooperative learning, and cognitive instruction. Although this approach began as a secondary level approach, its use has been expanded to other levels.

Strategy

A CALLA lesson is built around the following five steps:

1. Preparation—students' background knowledge and schemata about the content being studied as well as their learning strategies are explored

2. Presentation—the teacher presents the necessary new content and learning skills needed for the lesson

3. Practice—students perform various activities to reinforce the material to be learned

4. Evaluation—students evaluate their own learning

5. Expansion—students use what they have learned and apply it to new situations

Applications and Examples

A CALLA American History (Revolutionary War) Lesson

1. Students are given questions and exercises to help them and the teacher probe their background knowledge about the Revolutionary War. Students might be asked: What is a revolution? Has your country of origin had a revolution? Why do you think revolutions happen? Students might be shown pictures of the American Revolution's events and/or symbols and asked what they are looking at.

2. Students read about the American Revolution. Students are asked what they need to do to read the passage successfully. They look at the subheadings, pictures, and any preview or review questions to help them develop their learning strategies. They might be asked to predict what they think the text will be about. Students might also hear a lecture about the American Revolution, in which case, they would also be taught methods of note taking.

3. Students do exercises and activities related to the reading. They might answer questions about the reading, make a timeline of the events, make charts or tables to help them categorize information, or write sentences describing people or events of the Revolutionary War.

4. Students use a learning log to check what they know. Students mark off on a list the academic vocabulary they know, if they can use certain learning strategies, what they know about the Revolutionary War. They might also be asked questions such as: What was interesting about this

lesson? What was easy? What was difficult? How can you learn what is difficult? Students are encouraged to review information they don't know.

5. Students expand and apply their knowledge through various activities. Students might write about a famous Revolutionary War person. In groups students might debate the pros and cons of the Revolutionary War. Students might give presentations about a famous historical event in their country.

A Beginning Level CALLA Math Lesson

1. Students are shown different numbers and asked to say them in English as a review of numbers.

2. Students are then shown simple arithmetic problems and learn the words "addition," "subtraction," "multiplication," and "division."

3. Students then see a number of problems and are asked to say which operation (addition, subtraction, multiplication, division) they are seeing.

4. Students are given a worksheet that shows the different words used to express math operations such as "four plus four equals eight" or "eight minus six is two." Students are shown word problems and asked to say the problems.

5. Students are then given worksheets where they see word problems and write them out or see a problem written out and write it as a word problem. For example: The student sees $4 + 6 = 10$. The student writes: Four plus six equals ten. Or the student reads: Seven plus two equals nine. The student writes: $7 + 2 = 9$.

6. As an extension, students are asked to write problems using objects that they and their partners manipulate. For example, Chin has three books. He gives one book to Mohamed. They will write, "Three books minus one equals two books."

7. After students who are complete their activities, they will fill out a log that asks them what they learned, what they need to review, and what they else they need to know.

Weaknesses and Modifications

*   Students not in school may find academic content not relevant. However, the basic strategies of preparation, presentation, practice, evaluation, and expansion are applicable to many teaching situations.

See also: Content-based Second Language Instruction; Cooperative Learning; Language Experience Approach; Whole Language

Further Reading

Chamot, A. U., & O'Malley, J. M. (1994). *The CALLA handbook: Implementing the cognitive academic language learning approach.* Reading, MA: Addison-Wesley.

>   This is a thorough exploration of the CALLA approach with lots of ideas and examples for implementing the approach in various situations. It also includes information on assessment.

Chamot, A. U., O'Malley, J. M., & Kupper, L. (1992). *Building bridges: Content and learning strategies for ESL* (Books 1–3). Boston: Heinle & Heinle.

>   In this series of textbooks (beginning, intermediate, high intermediate) aimed at secondary level students and implementing the CALLA approach, chapters are content-based and include topics such as math, science, world civilizations, and literature.

Chamot, A. U., & O'Malley, J. M. (1992). The cognitive academic language learning approach: A bridge to the mainstream. In P. A. Richard-Amato & M. A. Snow (Eds.), *The multicultural classroom: Readings for content-area teachers.* Reading, MA: Addison-Wesley.

>   This is the formative article on this approach and has appeared in a number of journals.

Content-based Second Language Instruction

English Skill Level: All
Grade Level: All

Background

Content-based second language instruction (CBI) grew out of a response against curriculum built around grammar points. In CBI, the curriculum is built around a topic, theme, or subject area. Students learn another language via subject matter. CBI proponents believe that students are more likely to learn authentic and communicative language if they learn via content than if they just learn a set of grammar rules. In addition, students are more apt to be interested in language if it is contextualized and thus will learn it better. CBI has used a number of models, the three most common being a theme-based approach, sheltered classes, and adjunct classes (described below).

Strategy

Because content-based instruction is a broad approach, there are a number of strategies that can be used. One is the theme-based model. In this model:

1. A topic or theme is chosen that will be of interest and relevance to the whole class.

2. Activities then focus around the theme. For example, if the topic is the moon, the students might read both fiction and nonfiction literature about the moon; watch a video about it; practice numbers, distances, and measurements of it; learn about and use telescopes; study the history of moon exploration; learn about the phases of the moon; and study tidal activity on the earth.

3. Depending on the length of the unit, students might do only a few or several different activities and exercises related to the topic of the moon.

4. In addition to learning the content, students would also be taught the vocabulary and language structure that are compatible with such a topic.

5. Students practice writing and speaking in the target language about the topic.

Applications and Examples

Following are some theme-based lessons.

Body Language

1. The teacher asks the students if they know what the term "body language" means.

2. After discussing the definition, students are shown pictures of various gestures. They are asked, "What do these mean in your culture?" They are also asked what they think they mean in the United States. Students are asked for other examples.

3. Students read an article about body language.

4. After reading the article, students answer questions about the article and discuss whether body language has ever caused them difficulties.

5. Students review vocabulary learned so far.

6. Students review or are taught how to make the imperative (call a waiter, show you are hungry, tell someone you don't understand). Students are put into groups and think of situations in which members of the class might use body language. Students tell other students to use body language in certain situations.

7. In groups, students compare how gestures in certain cultures can have different meanings.

8. Students review or learn expressions of comparison such as "similar to," "different from," and "the same as."

9. Student groups present to the class some of the differences and similarities they have learned.

10. Students look back at the reading, and review some of the structures and vocabulary in the reading.

11. Students are assigned to write the first draft of a paper comparing body language between two cultures such as their own and the culture of the country they are visiting or to which they have moved.

Introduction to Psychology

1. Students are given an advice column to read.

2. Students are asked what they think of the problem in the advice column. Would they give the same advice? If not, what advice would they give? Do they think a psychologist would give the same advice? If not, what kind of advice might a psychologist give?

3. Students are asked to look for modals (can, should, must, had to, etc.) in the advice column.

4. Students are put into groups and asked to come up with a problem. They then ask the other groups for advice. Answers must be given using modals.

5. Students are given a longer passage from an introductory psychology book on the topic of frustration. Students preview the article by looking at the pictures, charts, and subheadings. Students read the article at home.

6. The next class period, students are asked if they have any questions about the article, including parts they did not understand.

7. Students are given activities to do that relate to the reading such as discussion questions, vocabulary questions, comprehension questions, outlining, and filling in graphic organizers.

8. In addition, students may view a video related to the topic. Students may take notes during the video and compare their notes with other class members.

9. Students are assigned to write about the topic of a frustrating experience they have had and what they did in reaction to that experience. To prepare for this writing assignment, students are put into groups to share stories of frustration with each other.

10. Students may also be given a test or quiz about the material they learned in class.

Apples

Submitted by Kelly Moen, Luther College education student

1. The teacher shows the students a picture of an apple orchard. The teacher also shows realia such as apples, apple seeds, and baskets. The teacher asks students what they know about apples and apple orchards:

    a. What do you see in the picture?

    b. Have you ever picked apples before?

      c.   How would you pick apples at the top of the tree?

      d.   Are the trees in this picture very young or several years old?

2. The teacher introduces students to planting and growing procedures. The teacher presents a chart to the class showing the stages of growth of a plant.

3. Students plant their own apple seeds.

4. Students are taken on a field trip to an apple orchard.

5. Students learn about the nutritional value of apples.

6. Students learn to read a recipe by making a treat from apples in class. For example, they might make apples dipped in caramel or apples with peanut butter.

7. Students write about what they have learned about apples.

Strengths

- Students are learning authentic language that is relevant to their needs.

Weaknesses

- Language teachers may not know enough about the content.
- Adjunct classes may take a lot of extra time that teachers do not have.

Modifications

- **Sheltered classes:** Sheltered classes are mainstream classes such as science, math, and language arts that are specifically geared toward students who are learning the target language. In these classes, the same content is taught as that in other mainstream classes, but special attention can be paid to particular problems that language-minority students may have such as vocabulary, language structure, and cultural contexts that may not be focused on in the mainstream class.

- **Adjunct classes:** In this model, students are enrolled in a concurrent content course and a support language course. Often the language teacher sits in on the content class to see what the students need to know and do. Then in the language support class, the language teacher can give extra support to help students understand the lecture and reading as well as help in writing reports, giving speeches, and other activities required in the content class. The content teacher and the language teacher may also work together so that the language teacher can prepare students beforehand about information and activities that will be covered in the content class.

See also: Cognitive Academic Language Learning Approach (CALLA); Communicative Approach; English for Academic Purposes; English for Specific Purposes

Further Reading

Brinton, D. M., & Master, R. P. (Eds.). (1997). *New ways in content-based instruction.* Alexandra, VA: TESOL.

    A volume in the New Ways Series, this book includes prescriptive lesson plans for teaching English language learners.

Brinton, D. M, Snow, M. A., & Wesche, M. B. (1989). *Content-based second language instruction.* Rowley, MA: Newbury House.
> The authors describe the principles of content-based instruction.

Brinton, D. M., Snow, M. A., & Wesche, M. B. (1993). Content-based second language instruction. In J. W. Oller (Ed.), *Methods that work: Ideas for literacy and language teachers* (2nd ed.). Boston: Heinle & Heinle.
> The paradigm of content-based instruction is explained.

Chamot, A. U., & O'Malley, J. M. (1994). Part three: Implementing CALLA in the classroom. In *The CALLA handbook: Implementing the cognitive academic language learning approach* (pp. 191–320). Reading, MA: Addison-Wesley.
> Details of CALLA are presented.

Crandall, J. (Ed.). (1995). *ESL through content-area instruction: Mathematics, science, social studies* (Language Education: Theory and Practice 67). McHenry, IL: Center for Applied Linguistics.
> The authors offer ideas on how to direct ESL instruction in math, science, and social studies classrooms.

Kasper, L. F. (Ed.). (2000). *Content-based college ESL instruction.* Mahwah, NJ: Lawrence Erlbaum Associates.
> Techniques of content-based ESL instruction are presented. A balance of theory and practice contribute to the readability and practicality of this resource.

Krashen, S. D. (1993). Sheltered subject-matter teaching. In J. W. Oller (Ed.), *Methods that work: Ideas for literacy and language teachers* (2nd ed.). Boston: Heinle & Heinle.
> Krashen's theory of second language acquisition is translated into methods applicable to the classroom setting.

McGarry, R. G. (1998). Professional writing for business administration: An adjunct, content-based course. *TESOL Journal, 7*(6), 28–31.
> McGarry suggests courses that integrated ESL and content-based instruction help learners to develop language skills as they gain knowledge in their courses.

Pally, M., & Bailey, N. (Eds.). (1999). *Sustained content teaching in academic ESL/EFL: A practical approach.* Boston: Houghton-Mifflin.
> Readers gain a general idea of the potential applications in classrooms of sustained content-based instruction in an ELL environment.

Richard-Amato, P. A., & Snow, M. A. (1996). A secondary sheltered English model. In *Making it happen: Interaction in the second language classroom* (pp. 334–338). Reading, MA: Addison-Wesley.
> The authors provide a brief description of sustained content teaching.

Sagliano, M., & Greenfield, K. (1998). A collaborative model of content-based EFL instruction in the liberal arts. *TESOL Journal, 7*(3), 23–28.
> Sagliano and Greenfield propose applying a content-based model in higher education for students learning English as a foreign language as they acquire knowledge in specific fields of study.

Snow, M. A. (2001). Content-based and immersion models for second and foreign language teaching. In M. Celce-Murcia (Ed.), *Teaching English as a second or foreign language* (3rd ed., pp. 303–318). Boston: Heinle & Heinle.
> Models for content-based instruction in teaching English as a second or foreign language are presented with practical ideas for teachers to follow.

Snow, M. A., & Brinton, D. M. (Eds.). (1997). *Content-based classroom: Perspectives on integrating language and content.* White Plains, NY: Longman.

   A thorough collection of articles covering all bases from specific instruction at various levels to assessment and research.

ESL Textbooks with a Content-based Instruction Approach

Bernache, C. (1994). *Gateway to achievement in the content areas.* New York: McGraw-Hill/Contemporary.

Brinton, D. (1997). *Insights: A content-based approach to academic preparation.* White Plains, NY: Longman.

Chamot, A. U. (1999). *America: The early years (up to the 1800's).* White Plains, NY: Longman.

Chamot, A. U. (1999). *America: After independence (1800–1900).* White Plains, NY: Longman.

Christison, M. A., & Bassano, S. (1997). *Earth and physical science: Content and learning strategies.* Reading, MA: Longman.

Christison, M. A., & Bassano, S. (1997). *Life science: Content and learning strategies.* Reading, MA: Longman.

Christison, M. A., & Bassano, S. (1997). *Social studies: Content and learning strategies.* Reading, MA: Longman.

Connerton, P., & Reid, F. (1997). *Linkages: A content-based integrated skills program.* Heinle & Heinle.

DeFilippo, J., & Skidmore, C. (2004). *Skill sharpener* (2nd ed.). White Plains, NY: Longman.

Espeseth, M. (1996). *Academic listening encounters: Listening, note taking, and discussion, content focus: Human behavior.* New York: Cambridge University Press.

Gomez, S., et al. (1995). *Eureka: Science demonstrations for ESL classes.* Reading, MA: Addison-Wesley.

Iwamoto, J. R. (1994) *Coming together, book 1: Integrating math and language in a sheltered approach to mathematics for secondary students.* White Plains, NY: Longman.

Iwamoto, J. R. (1994) *Coming together, book 2: Integrating math and language in a sheltered approach to mathematics for secondary students.* White Plains, NY: Longman.

Kauffman, D., & Apple, G. (2000). *The Oxford picture dictionary for the content areas.* New York: Oxford University Press.

Lubawy, S. (2000). *World view: A global study of geography, history, and culture.* Palatine, IL: Linmore.

Nelson, V. (1999). *Building skills for social studies: Reading skills, writing skills, communication skills, math skills, map skills, charting & graphing skills, science skills, timeline skills.* New York: McGraw-Hill/Contemporary.

Seal, B. (1996). *Academic encounters: Reading, study skills, and writing, content focus: Human behavior.* New York: Cambridge University Press.

Terdy, D. (1986). *Content area ESL: Social studies.* Palatine, IL: Linmore.

Zimmerman, F. (1989). *English for science.* White Plains, NY: Longman.

English for Academic Purposes

English Skill Level: Advanced Beginning to Advanced
Grade Level: Upper Elementary to Adult

Background

English for academic purposes (EAP) has been developed to teach precollege or college-level students the necessary skills and vocabulary needed to be successful at the college and university level. Such an approach is often used in intensive programs associated with colleges and universities. Traditional curriculum in this approach has often been built around the discrete language skills of reading, writing, listening, speaking, and sometimes grammar and vocabulary. More recently other programs have become more integrated or built around academic content areas. Academic skills may include teaching students to give speeches, write research papers, work in groups, read academic texts, for example. Students learn not only the English to go with these tasks, but also the discourse and rhetorical patterns specific to the target academic culture. Although vocabulary and language structure may focus on specific fields, focus is often on vocabulary and structure that is common to all academic fields as well.

Strategy

Although there is no one specific way to approach English for Academic Purposes, most programs try to focus their curriculum around the skills and content that students will use in their college or university classes.

1. Teachers conduct a needs analysis of the academic skills, content, discourse, and vocabulary which students will need to be successful in an academic setting.

2. Teachers consider the following questions:

    a. Will the program be built around content or discrete skills?

    b. Are the students undergraduates, graduates, or a mix?

    c. Are the students in one field only or several different ones?

    d. Will students be only in EAP classes, or will they also be taking regular academic classes?

    e. How will the teacher decide when students' English and academic skills are good enough to meet the demands of the college or university?

3. From the information obtained from the needs analysis as well as answers to these questions, the teacher designs a curriculum that provides the students with what they will need to know in an academic setting. The content of the curriculum might include topics such as science, psychology, and business. Skill areas might include giving speeches, reading textbooks, writing papers, working in groups, listening to lectures, and taking notes.

4. Teachers develop assessment instruments that will give them and other concerned parties the information needed to feel confident that students will be successful when they enter their field of study.

Applications and Examples

An Intermediate Speaking and Listening Class in a Discrete-Skills Program

The focus of the class is the topic of space exploration. Students are given a short exercise that lists famous events in space exploration such as when the telescope was invented, when Pluto was discovered, when the first space flight took place, when a human first walked on the moon. Students are asked to match dates with the events. As a class, students guess the dates to see if they know the answer. Students are asked if they think space exploration is a good thing and why or why not. These introductory exercises are used to discover and highlight students' knowledge about space. In addition, vocabulary or concepts that students may need to know for the upcoming lecture can be previewed. Students listen to a fairly brief lecture about space. This lecture might be given by the teacher, be on video, or be on audiocassette. Students listen only to the lecture the first time. The second time, as students listen they fill in the missing information in an outline. Students may compare their answers with other students or check their answers on an overhead the teacher displays. Students then listen a third time so they can attend again to those parts they had difficulty understanding.

Students are asked what they think living in space would be like. Students are then put in groups and given time to design a space colony. Students plan and draw their colony. Once students have designed their space colony, they give a presentation about it to the rest of the class. Students can be reminded about the use of the future and the conditional tenses for their presentation. Other students ask questions about the students' colonies. Then students are asked which colony they would like to live on and why. The teacher or the students (or both together) can fill out an assessment form evaluating the students' presentations.

An Integrated Skills Course for Graduate Students Already Enrolled in Some Academic Classes

The semester course is divided up into academic topics such as demography, applied linguistics, biological sciences, marketing, and computer technology. For each academic topic, students break into groups for about a two- to three-week period and practice working in groups. Students are given information on how to disagree politely, how to make a point, how to interrupt another speaker, and so on. Students are given tasks to complete. For example, students may develop a plan for a business they hope to develop. They will do research on their line of business. They may present their plan to others to get support. This includes putting necessary information on graphs, tables, and charts and being able to explain the information. Students write up their results.

In addition, throughout the semester students will do individual projects related to their field of study. For example, graduate students may give a twenty-minute presentation on an aspect of their field that will be understood by a general academic audience. Students will also practice listening to lectures and note taking. Students will also be guided in writing academic material such as summaries, essays, and research papers. Throughout the semester students will be required to hand in various parts of their research paper such as an abstract, a thesis statement, an outline, and several rough drafts checked for structure, vocabulary, and organization and coherence. This paper can be a real paper they are writing for one of their university classes. In fact, as often as possible, assignments are related to what is actually going on in their university classes. Students are evaluated through tests that include multiple-choice questions, short-answer questions, and essay questions so that students may practice the types of exams they will likely encounter in their academic classes.

Weaknesses and Modifications

- Because EAP focuses on the particular needs of students in higher education, those students not involved in or planning on continuing their academic studies may find the academic orientation irrelevant or even boring.

From *A Kaleidoscope of Models and Strategies for Teaching English to Speakers of Other Languages* by Deborah L. Norland, Ph.D. and Terry Pruett-Said. Westport, CT: Libraries Unlimited/Teacher Ideas Press. Copyright © 2006.

- Modifications can be made if you have a mix of students by including topics that all foreign language students will encounter, such as shopping, numbers, finance, and transportation.

See also: Content-based Second Language Instruction; English for Specific Purposes

Further Reading

Ferris, D., & Tagg, T. (1996). Academic listening/speaking tasks for ESL students: Problems, suggestions, and implications. *TESOL Quarterly, 30*(2), 297–317.

    The authors concentrate on the views of college and university professors on the challenges of their ESL students with speaking and listening English language tasks. Professors generally believe that students are less proficient with academic English than conversational "everyday" listening and speaking.

Flowerdew, J., & Peacock, M. (2001) *Research perspectives on English for academic purposes.* Cambridge, England: Cambridge University Press.

    This collection of articles begins with a discussion of the social and political aspects of EAP and continues with an exploration of research in curriculum design in EAP situations.

Grabe, W., & Stoller, F. L. (2001). *Teaching English as a second or foreign language* (3rd ed.). Boston: Heinle & Heinle.

    This article discusses the importance of reading in EAP with guidelines for creating an effective EAP reading curriculum.

Jordan, R. (1997). *English for academic purposes: A guide and resource book for teachers.* Cambridge, England: Cambridge University Press.

    Jordan provides a thorough coverage of the background of EAP with information on EAP syllabus design and more specific EAP areas such as academic reading and writing, academic speaking, and vocabulary development.

Pally, M. (2000). *Sustained content teaching in academic ESL/EFL.* Boston: Houghton-Mifflin.

    This collection of articles gives different examples of EAP instruction through content. Topics include writing for engineering students, U.S. history, health, and information on assessment in sustained content teaching.

Journals

Journal of English for Academic Purposes

    Information available at http://www.elsevier.com/locate/jeap

English for Specific Purposes

English Skill Level: Intermediate to Advanced
Grade Level: Secondary to Adult

Background

As English became a lingua franca worldwide, particularly in fields such as business and science, there developed a need to focus on the language needs of those people using English as an international language and to develop programs specifically to meet their needs. English for Specific Purposes (ESP) classes focus on both the structure and lexis needed for a particular field as well as the types of activities that the student is expected to perform within the profession.

Strategy

1. The first step in ESP is to do a needs analysis of the field or profession in which the students will be working.

2. From the needs analysis, find the activities that the students will be required to do in English within their field. Activities might include giving speeches, reading journals, conducting board meetings, and so on.

3. Also include in the curriculum vocabulary, structure, spoken discourse, and rhetorical patterns that are specific to the students' field and future tasks.

Applications and Examples

Creating a Small Business

This activity could be used either for business students or art and design students.

1. Students are put into groups.

2. As a group, students decide which small business they would like to start. They might choose a restaurant, a travel agency, a clothing store, or any other small business.

3. Students decide what will need to be done to start a small business such as:

    a. How to find funding

    b. Where to locate the business

    c. How to advertise

    d. How to design and decorate the establishment

    The areas of focus might depend on the specialty of the students. For example, business students might decide to concentrate on the financial aspects of the business, whereas art and design students might decide to concentrate on the design of advertising and the establishment.

4. Each group of students presents its business plan to the other students in the class, who can respond to the plan as potential investors might. The other students should be encouraged to ask questions of the presenting group regarding the business plan. Finally, the "investors" can explain why they would or would not approve the plan.

Preparing to Write about Art

This lesson teaches students art terminology and descriptive adjectives to help them write a critique of a piece of art.

1. Students are introduced to the art design elements of line, shape, space, light, color, and texture through the viewing of visual representations that show different uses of the elements.

2. Students are given a reproduction of a painting and asked to analyze its design elements. Students can present their analysis orally or in writing.

3. Students choose different pages of a text that describes a piece of art. Students underline or write the descriptive adjectives. Students share their words with the class while the teacher writes them on the board.

4. The teacher then shows students a variety of art reproductions. For each reproduction, students must give one or two descriptive adjectives. Students cannot repeat what other students have said. This is to encourage students to come up with more words that can be used to describe the same object.

5. Students are then assigned to write a description of a piece of art.

Strengths

• Students' real and specific needs are met.

• Authentic materials are used.

• ESP courses tend to be short and intense because of the narrow focus.

Weaknesses

• Classes may be so narrowly focused that the broader needs of some students are not met.

• The time, effort, and cooperation needed to do a good needs analysis may not always be available.

Further Reading

Douglas, D. (2000). *Assessing languages for specific purposes.* Cambridge, England: Cambridge University Press.

    A discussion of testing that focuses on assessing language used in specific situations as opposed to testing for general purposes. It includes a discussion of some tests that are already made for that purpose. Part of the Cambridge Language Assessment Series.

Dudley-Evans, T. (2001). English for specific purposes. In R. Carter & D. Nunan (Eds.), *The Cambridge guide to teaching English to speakers of other languages* (pp. 131–136.) Cambridge, England: Cambridge University Press.

    This brief article defines ESP with particular attention to needs analysis and text analysis.

Dudley-Evans, T., & St. John, M. J. (1998). *Developments in ESP: A multi-disciplinary approach.* Cambridge, England: Cambridge University Press.

    In this book, the authors offer a discussion of why and how to assess language used for specific purposes as opposed to general language tests.

Holme, R. (1996) *ESP ideas: Recipes for teaching academic and professional English.* Canterbury, England: Pilgrims/Longman UK.

> In this collection of teacher-friendly activities, the authors organize the content under general areas of expertise such as negotiating, data mapping, reasoning out a problem, and getting across a point.

Hutchinson, T., & Waters, A. (1987). *English for specific purposes: A learning-centred approach.* Cambridge, England: Cambridge University Press.

> The authors' thorough exploration of ESP covers definition of the approach, course design, application, and the role of the ESP teacher.

Johns, A. M., & Price-Machado, D. (2001). English for specific purposes: Tailoring courses to student needs—and to the outside world. In M. Celce-Murcia (Ed.), *Teaching English as a second or foreign language* (3rd ed., pp. 43–54). Boston: Heinle and Heinle.

> This article defines ESP and discusses how to prepare an ESP curriculum including different methods of needs assessment.

Master, P., & Brinton, D. (Eds.). (1998). *New ways in English for specific purposes.* Alexandria, VA: TESOL.

> Master and Brinton provide collection of lessons for the ESP areas of EAP, art and design, business and economics, legal purposes, science and technology, and vocational purposes.

Wilberg, P. (1987*). One to one: A teacher's handbook.* Hove, England: Language Teaching Publications.

> Although the main purpose of this book is explaining how to teach one on one, it has many good ideas on how to create lessons aimed at students involved with English for specific purposes.

Lexical Approach

English Skill Level: Advanced Beginning to Advanced
Grade Level: Upper Elementary to Adult

Background

The lexical approach was developed by Michael Lewis (*The Lexical Approach,* 1993) who believes that the primary approach in foreign language teaching should be focused on the lexicon (vocabulary) of the language as opposed to using the more traditional grammatical or structural approach. He also believes that vocabulary needs to be taught directly as rather than through natural and communicative approaches that propose vocabulary will be learned inductively as students become exposed to the target language. His main thesis is that vocabulary should be taught in "chunks" instead of as individual words. These chunks are referred to as *collocations.* That is, words that frequently go together, such as "ancient history" not "old history" or "former history" should be learned together. Followers of the lexical approach frequently make use of concordances, computer programs that can scan large amounts of material for use of specific words and their collocations. Such information can also be found in concordance dictionaries.

Strategy

1. Students are introduced to the concept of collocations. The teacher may do this as certain words and their collocations come up in lessons. Or teachers may give students a list of words and ask them to find them in a text as well as the words they go with. Teachers may also introduce collocations by making word charts that show with which other words the others can be used. Students may also be introduced to concordance programs on computers.

2. Once students are introduced to the concept of collocations, they can continue improving on this by keeping their own notebooks with lists of words and their collocations (see example that follows).

3. Students can also do various exercises or writing assignments in which they are asked to produce to recognize and then produce certain collocations.

Applications and Examples

Keeping a Collocation Notebook

In some ways, collocation notebooks are similar to the vocabulary notebooks that many students learning other languages keep. In a collocation notebook, however, there are few individual words listed. Instead, students keep track of words that go together with other words such as collocations and fixed expressions. The teacher may make photocopied sheets that students can use, or students can develop their own organizational system. Some collocation categories that are useful are the following:

- Verbs that go with certain nouns (do homework, finish homework, complete homework, correct homework, hand in homework)

- Adjectives that go with certain nouns (hard work, interesting work)

- Noun + noun (transport costs, overhead costs, labor costs)

- Verb + adverb (drive fast, drive carefully)

- Expressions (I should *emphasize* that, I should *point out* that, I should *remind* you that)

Students may learn collocations as they are reading or listening. Teachers may ask students to look for collocations in a reading. Other students may add their own collocations when they know them. Teachers can also give lists of collocations to students as they come up in class. Students may locate collocations in collocation dictionaries or in concordance programs as well.

Collocation Exercise

- Students can be asked to identify which words go with other words.
- Student can finish set expressions.
- Students can be given cards with nouns, verbs, adjectives, and adverbs and asked to create expressions or sentences with the words on those cards.

Further Reading

DeCarrico, J. S. (2001). Vocabulary learning and teaching. In Celce-Murcia (Ed.), *Teaching English as a second or foreign language* (3rd ed., pp. 285–299). Boston: Heinle & Heinle.
> This chapter presents an explanation of lexical competence relative to communicative competence.

Fox, G. (1998). Using corpus data in the classroom. In B. Tomlinson (Ed.), *Materials development in language teaching* (pp. 25–43). Cambridge, England: Cambridge University Press.
> Fox's article shows several examples of concordances and various ways such information can be used in the classroom.

Lewis, M. (1997). *Implementing the lexical approach: Putting theory into practice.* Hove, England: Language Teaching Publications.
> Lewis offers ideas that promote developing students' ability with words and word combinations.

Lewis, M. (Ed.). (2000). *Teaching collocation: Further developments in the lexical approach.* Hove, England: Language Teaching Publications.
> Lewis explains how language is learned based on theory supporting the lexical approach.

Nation, P. (Ed.). (1995). *New ways in teaching vocabulary.* Alexandra, VA: Teachers of English to Students of Other Languages (TESOL).
> Innovative ideas in teaching English to speakers of other languages using the lexical approach are explained.

Nattinger, J. R., & DeCarrico, J. S. (1992). *Lexical phrases and language teaching.* Oxford, England: Oxford University Press.
> Includes a thorough discussion of lexical phrases and examples of how to teach with them.

Schmitt, N., & Carter, R. (2000). The lexical advantages of narrow reading for second language learners. *TESOL Journal, 9*(1), 4– 9.
> This article explains the use of concordances.

Wichman, A., Fligelstone, S., McEnery, T., & Knowles, G. (Eds.). (1997). *Teaching and language corpora.* London: Longman
> This collection of articles focuses largely on the computer side of corpora (collection of linguistic data).

Willis, J. (1998). Concordances in the classroom without a computer: Assembling and exploiting concordances of common words. In B. Tomlinson (Ed.), *Materials development in language teaching* (pp. 44–66). Cambridge, England: Cambridge University Press.
> The authors explain how students can create their own lexical phrases and linguistic features without the use of a computer.

Competency-based Approach

English Skill Level: Beginning to Advanced
Grade Level: Upper Elementary to Adult

Background

Competency-based education (CBE), an approach to adult and literacy education, began to be used in adult education ESL in the 1970s. Competency-based ESL is centered around teaching to competencies. A competency is a task-based goal to be met by the learner. Competencies frequently include basic survival skills like taking transportation, going to the doctor, and buying necessities. However, competencies could also be goals to be met by students or professionals. A competency-based approach includes an assessment of learners' needs, selection of competencies based on those needs, instruction targeted on meeting those needs, and evaluation of learners' performance in meeting the competencies. A competency-based approach continues to be the primary method used in U.S. government–funded adult education ESL programs. The two most widely known competency based programs in the United States are (1) SCANS, which is the Secretary's Commission on Achieving Necessary Skills, a report put out in 1991 by the U.S. government detailing what competencies, skills, and personal qualities are needed to succeed in the workplace, and (2) CASAS (Comprehensive Adult Student Assessment System), a private organization that has created its own competencies with its own materials and assessment and is now used by a number of adult education programs in the United States. In addition, CBE is also used extensively in Australian adult ESL programs for immigrants.

Strategy

1. The teacher conducts a needs assessment to see how and where students will need to use English to be successful in the future.

2. The teacher defines tasks, or competencies, that students will need to accomplish. Examples of competencies might include requesting and giving personal information, asking for the time, practicing transactions in the post office, and making a doctor's appointment.

3. The teacher creates lessons and activities that will teach students how to accomplish the tasks, or competencies, that have been prescribed. Lessons might include new vocabulary, understanding and practicing dialogues, reading and filling out forms, and discussing previous experiences and future problems that might occur.

4. Students are evaluated on their ability to perform the designated task or competency.

Applications and Examples

Shopping for Clothes

1. A picture of a clothing store with a clerk and a woman is shown to students. Students are asked, "What is happening in this picture?" If students have difficulty answering, the teacher can ask more direct questions: "Where are they?" "Who is this woman?" "What is she doing?" Students are then asked about their shopping experiences with questions such as, "Do you like to shop?" "What do you like to buy?" "Where do you shop?" "How often do you shop?" Such questions not only help students focus on the topic but also help the teacher assess what the students know and what they need to know.

2. Students are then shown pictures of different articles of clothing. Students review the names and colors of articles of clothing.

3. Students then listen to a dialogue between the shopper and the store clerk. Students may follow the written dialogue as they listen.

Clerk:	Can I help you?
Shopper:	Yes, I'm looking for a new dress to wear to work.
Clerk:	What size do you wear?
Shopper:	I wear a size 12.
Clerk:	What color would you like?
Shopper:	I'd like something in blue.
Clerk:	How about this dress?
Shopper:	No, I don't really care for that dress.
Clerk:	How about this one?
Shopper:	Yes, I like that one.
Clerk:	Would you like to try it on?
Shopper:	Yes, where is the dressing room?

(Shopper tries on the dress)

Clerk:	How does it fit?
Shopper:	Just fine. I think I'll get it.

Note: Within the dialogue are a number of idiomatic expressions that are used when shopping.

4. The teacher points out new vocabulary in the dialogue such as

Looking for

Size

How about

Don't care for

Try it on

Dressing room

Does it fit

I'll get it

5. Students practice parts of the dialogues. First, students practice saying individual lines as a class. Then students practice the dialogue in pairs. Then students practice shopping in pairs using the practice dialogue or their own. Students then role-play the situation.

6. Once students can accomplish this competency, they can go on to similar competencies such as shopping for groceries, buying clothes for children, shopping in a hardware store. Students can also go on to other topics such as going to the doctor, applying for a job, or visiting with their children's teachers.

See also: Learner-Centered Approach; Vocational English as a Second Language

Further Reading

Auerbach, E. R. (1986). Competency-based ESL: One step forward or two steps back? *TESOL Quarterly, 20*(3), 411–429.

>   Auerbach examines the underlying principles of competency-based ESL programs. According to Auerbach, competency-based programs focus on life skills and are based on mutually agreed-on, continually assessed performance outcomes.

CASAS Competency List. Retrieved from http://www.casas.org/01AboutCasas/Complist2003.pdf
    The CASAS Web site explains the system and provides information about the competencies, instructional resources, and training opportunities.

Peyton, J., & Crandall, J. (1995). *Philosophies and approaches in adult ESL literacy instruction.* Retrieved May 3, 2006, from http://www.ericdigest.org/1996-2/esl.html
    The Web site for the Center for Applied Linguistics contains a plethora of information about a variety of approaches for teaching English language learners.

Richards, J. C., & Rodgers, T. S. (2001). *Competency-based language teaching in approaches and methods in language teaching* (2nd ed., pp. 141–150). Cambridge, England: Cambridge University Press.
    The authors provide a good summary covering the history, theory, and current use of this approach.

U.S. Department of Labor. (1993). *Teaching the SCANS competencies.* ERIC Document ED 354 400.
    This document discusses the influence the SCANS or the Secretary's Commission on Achieving Necessary Skills, the U.S. Department of Labor report on educational reform.

Whetzel, D. (1992). *The Secretary of Labor's Commission on Achieving Necessary Skills.* ERIC Document ED339749.
    This ERIC document describes the process used to identify the basic skills listed in SCANS.

ESL Textbooks Correlated to Competencies Such as SCANS, CASAS, and Other State-Level Competencies

Brown, D. H. (1998). *New vistas.* White Plains, NY: Longman.

Burton, E. (1995). *Going places: Picture-based English.* White Plains, NY: Longman.

Carver, T. K., & Fotinos, S. D. (1997). *A conversation book* (books 1 and 2). White Plains, NY: Longman.

Chamot, A. U., et al. (2000). *Perspectives 2000* (books 1 and 2). Boston: Heinle & Heinle.

Foley, B. H., & Neblett, E. R. (2003) *The new grammar in action: An integrated course in English.* Boston: Heinle & Heinle.

Foley, B. H., & Pomann, H. (1982) *Lifelines: Coping skills in English, books.* White Plains, NY: Longman.

Harris, T. (1995). *Exploring English. A. Rowe, Illustrator.* White Plains, NY: Longman.

Jenkins, R., & Sabbagh, S. L. (2001). *Stand out: Standards-based English* (books 1–4). Boston: Heinle & Heinle.

Kerwin, M. (1995). *Topics and language competencies.* White Plains, NY: Prentice Hall.

Magy, R. (1998). *Working it out: Interactive English for the workplace.* Boston: Heinle & Heinle.

Molinsky, S. J., & Bliss, B. (1995). *Expressways.* White Plains, NY: Longman.

Molinsky, S. J., & Bliss, B. (2000). *Side by side* (3rd ed.). White Plains, NY: Longman.

Nunan, D. (2001) *Expressions: Meaningful English communication.* Boston: Heinle & Heinle.

Price-Machado, D. (1998). *Skills for success: Working and studying in English.* New York: Cambridge University Press.

Saslow, J., & Collins, T. (2001). *Workplace plus.* White Plains, NY: Longman.

Weinstein-Shr, G., & Huizenga, J. (1996). *Collaborations: English in our lives, a 5-level series.* Boston: Heinle & Heinle.

Critical Pedagogy

English Skill Level: Advanced Beginning to Advanced
Grade Level: Secondary to Adult
Also Called: Critical Literacy, Participatory ESL, Problem-Posing Education

Background

Critical literacy is a teaching orientation that focuses on encouraging students to analyze critically a text's purpose and the culture and power structure it represents. It also encourages students to choose issues for their classroom study that have real meaning in their own lives. Paulo Friere, a Brazilian educator, is often viewed as the founder of this orientation (*Pedagogy of the Oppressed,* 1970). He believed that education and knowledge could only have power when they help learners liberate themselves from oppressive conditions. Although some approaches to critical literacy only ask students to come away with a better understanding of society and their role in it, other approaches encourage students to go a step further and become activists in their own communities.

Strategy

1. The teacher encourages students and listens as they discuss their everyday lives.

2. The teacher facilitates open discussion and encourages students to express concerns.

3. The teacher assesses students' situation to help them determine topics that truly concern them.

4. The teacher chooses a picture, story, or song to present to students to help them take an objective look at their experiences and concerns.

5. Students meet in small groups, called culture circles, to discuss and propose a project related to their concerns.

6. Students plan a project, which often includes social action, to improve their situation.

Applications and Examples

My Neighborhood

1. The teacher asks students, "What do you do everyday?" Students answer and may also ask other students. The teacher helps students with vocabulary and structure as students talk about their typical day. The teacher and other students can ask students more questions about their day, including questions about what they like to do and why or what they don't like to do and why.

2. The teacher shows a picture of a city neighborhood. He or she asks students what they see. Again, the teacher helps students with vocabulary and structure as needed. The teacher then asks students, "What do you like about this neighborhood?" "What don't you like about it?" "What does your neighborhood look like?" "What do you like about your neighborhood?" "What don't you like about?"

3. Students, together or in groups, decide on a problem they want to solve in their neighborhoods. They may do this as a class project to be presented to their teacher and the other students, or they may decide to continue with their project outside of class.

Diversity in Our Town

Submitted by Becky Sutter, Luther College education student

1. The objective of this lesson is for learners to observe and discuss the amount of help that different public places provide for people who speak languages other than English. The learner identifies various ways that public places could be more helpful to people who speak languages other than English.

2. During the week before the lesson, the teacher encourages the students to pay attention to things that public institutions do or do not do to make it easier for people who speak a language other than English. Students should look for signs written in other languages, for pictures, and for diagrams. Students should also look to see whether public institutions like schools, doctor's offices, and stores have bilingual employees. The teacher could also bring in pamphlets and other materials put out by various institutions for students to analyze.

3. The teacher begins the lesson by reading *Marianthe's Story: Painted Words/Spoken Memories* by Aliki (Greenwillow Books, 1998). This is a book in two parts about a girl who immigrates to the United States. She shares her story of the difficulties she faced in her first days in a classroom where everyone speaks a different language from hers. The teacher asks the students the following questions:

    a. What were some problems that Marianthe had when she didn't understand the language that her teacher and friends were speaking?

    b. What things were hard for her to understand?

    c. What things could she understand?

    d. How did she communicate?

4. The teacher asks the students if they ever felt like Marianthe and asks them to share stories of times when they or their family have had problems because of language barriers. For those students who may feel uncomfortable discussing their own difficulties, this part of the discussion should be optional.

5. The teacher will ask students to get into preassigned heterogeneous small groups. The teacher instructs the students to discuss observations that they made over the week about how public institutions do or do not provide help for non-English speakers.

6. Students construct a chart of their observations as follows:

Helpful	**Not Helpful**
Wells Fargo Banks has signs in Spanish, Hmong, and English	Johnson Health Care has no doctors or translators who speak Spanish

7. The teacher asks each group to think of solutions to their observations listed in the "Not Helpful" column.

8. In a follow-up lesson, students write a letter to one of the institutions that they identified as nonhelpful, giving suggestions on how it could better serve non-English speakers. Students are given the option of whether to mail the letter.

Analyzing a Text for Bias

1. Students are given a newspaper article about a current event or a topic that concerns them. The article is previewed by looking at the title, any subtitles, and the pictures. Students are asked what they know about this and what they think about this topic.

2. Students read the article more thoroughly. They are asked to write down what they think are facts and what they think are opinions. More advanced students can be asked to point out terms that show bias or emotional overdramatization. Students are asked their opinions about the topic. They are asked their opinion about the writing. Is it fair? Is it biased? What has been left out? What should have been included?

3. Students, individually, in groups, or as a class, write a letter to the editor responding to the article. Students may decide whether they want to send the letter to the newspaper.

Strengths

*   Instruction is grounded in the experiences of students and teachers, not a standardized curriculum controlled by textbook publishers, teachers, and administrators.

*   Meaningful conversation is the norm because the dialogue is based on the experiences of students and teachers.

*   Students are partners with teachers in learning.

Weaknesses and Modifications

*   Some students may be uncomfortable discussing issues that are too personal or too political. Teachers should try to keep the discussion at an objective, general level so that students do not feel compelled to discuss personal issues if they do not wish to do so. Students should never be put on the spot nor should they be required to go public with activities unless they desire to attend them.

See also: Learner-Centered Approach

Further Reading

Auerbach, E. R. (1992). *Making meaning, making change: Participatory curriculum development for adult ESL literacy.* Washington, DC: Center for Applied Linguistics.

   This is the classic text by one of the leading proponents of the participatory approach in adult education ESL.

Auerbach, E. R. (1996). *Adult ESL/literacy from the community to the community: A guidebook for participatory literacy training.* Mahwah, NJ: Lawrence Erlbaum Associates.

   A teaching manual presenting several real-life programs of where the participants in adult education became the teachers.

Auerbach, E. R. (2001). "Yes, but…": Problematizing participatory ESL pedagogy. In P. Campbell & B. Burnaby (Eds.), *Participatory practices in adult education* (pp. 287–305). Mahwah, NJ: Lawrence Erlbaum Associates.

   This article presents some of the arguments or dilemmas that have been posed by those that have practiced participatory pedagogy with Auerbach's answers and suggestions.

Hones, D. F. (1999). US Justice? Critical pedagogy and the case of Mumia Abu-Jamal. *TESOL Journal, 8*(4), 27–33.

   This article presents the details of an in-class ESL course using critical literacy and content-based instruction as its guidelines.

Morgan, B. D. (1998). *The ESL classroom: Teaching, critical practice, and community development*. Toronto: University of Toronto Press.

    This text provides an integrated approach to teaching English to adult learners. The book explores the necessity of including social and political issues in language education and the "site of transformation" that language learning provides. Lesson plans for the intermediate to advanced adult ESL learner are included.

Shore, I. (1987). *Friere for the classroom*. Portsmouth, NH: Heineman.

    An anthology of essays by teachers using Paulo Freire's methodology in their classrooms.

TESOL Quarterly (1999). *TESOL Quarterly 33*(3).

    The entire issue of the journal is devoted to critical pedagogy.

Van Duzer, C., & Cunningham Florez, M. A. (1999). *Critical literacy for adult English language learners*. Washington, DC: National Clearinghouse for ESL Literacy Education (EDO-LE-99-07). Retrieved from http://www.cal.org/caela/esl_resources/digests/critlit.html

    This is an overview of an argument for critical literacy. Activities and strategies for using the theory in the classroom are provided.

Wink, J. (1997). *Critical pedagogy: Notes from the real world*. Los Angeles: California Association of Bilingual Education.

    Wink provides an analysis and argument for critical pedagogy and how it opens the door to broader and deeper perspectives.

Wolfe, P. M. (1996). Literacy bargains: Toward a critical literacy in a multilingual classroom. *TESOL Journal, 5*(4), 22–26.

    Wolfe's article presents the steps involved in setting up a lesson in which high school students use the critical literacy approach to analyze shopping malls.

Family Literacy

English Skill Level: All
Grade Level: All

Background

Family literacy is based on the belief and related research that students will be more successful in school if their parents prepare and support them. Family literacy was first developed to prepare emergent readers for school success by giving information and activities that parents could use with their children to help support their literacy efforts. During the 1980s, family literacy activities became a part of the ESL curriculum in both adult education ESL programs and K–12. As ESL family literacy programs evolved, it became apparent that schools also needed to learn about the cultures and beliefs of the multicultural communities they were serving. Thus, at least in ESL programs, family literacy is viewed as a two-way process (Auerbach, 1989). Some activities may include having parents and children learn about the U.S. education system and the expectations of their particular school system. Other activities may include having parents read or tell traditional stories to their children, having children read stories to their parents in English or their native language, or having families create videos or Web pages about themselves and their communities.

Strategies

Family literacy can include any number of approaches and activities. The following strategies give some general guidelines.

1. Complete a needs analysis that includes both the perceived needs of the school system as well as the strengths, beliefs, and needs of the community being served. One approach to discover the needs of the community is to meet with local leaders. Another way is to be aware of the concerns of the community that may be expressed in students' writing or discussions.

2. Develop activities and programs that meet the needs of all concerned, including parents, students, teachers, and other members of the school and community.

3. Assess activities and programs to see if they are really meeting the needs of all concerned and fostering an environment that helps students achieve in school.

Weaknesses and Modifications

- Parents and guardians are actively involved in the education of their children.

- Parents and guardians may participate in shared learning experiences, thus conveying the message to their children that education is valid.

Weaknesses and Modifications

- Family literacy programs that come only from the top down may prove unsuccessful if they conflict with the culture and practices of the group being served. Therefore, it is important that family literacy programs include the needs and practices of everyone involved.

- Individual teachers may not be in the position to create family literacy programs, but they can use some of the activities used in established programs to develop connections between the classroom, students, and parents.

See also: Critical Pedagogy; Whole Language

Further Reading

Auerbach, E. (1989). Toward a socio-contextual approach to family literacy. *Harvard Educational Review, 59,* 165–181.

>This article suggests that schools need to learn about the cultures and beliefs of the multicultural communities they are serving. Thus, at least in ESL programs, family literacy is viewed as a two-way process.

Holt, D. H., & Van Duzer, C. H. (Eds.). (2000). *Assessing success in family literacy and adult ESL.* Washington, DC: Center for Applied Linguistics and Delta Systems.

>This collection of articles looks at the use of alternative assessment and evaluation in literacy and adult education ESL programs.

Hurley, S. R., & Tinajero, V. J. (2001). *Literacy assessment of second language learners.* Boston: Allyn & Bacon.

>This collection of articles focuses on K–12. It discusses and gives examples of various assessment activities that can be used with second language learners.

Journal of Educational Issues of Language Minority Students, 16. (1996, Summer). [Special issue].

>This special issue of the journal focuses on parental involvement.

Morrow, L. M. (Ed.). (1995). *Family literacy: Connections in schools and communities.* New Brunswick, NJ: Rutgers University Press.

>A collection of articles that explore various practices and programs in family literacy collected in response to Barbara Bush's initiative on family literacy.

Morrow, L. M., Tracey, D. H., & Maxwell, C. M. (Eds.). (1995). *A survey of family literacy in the United States.* Newark, DE: International Reading Association.

>This sourcebook lists numerous examples of family literacy programs for both native and nonnative speakers with short descriptions of each. There is also information on research taking place and agencies that are involved in family literacy.

Taylor, D. (Ed.). (1997). *Many families, many literacies: An international declaration of principles.* Portsmouth, NH: Heinemann.

>This collection of articles focuses on the principles that family literacy programs should follow. It includes sections on assessment, research, pedagogy, funding, and policy.

Weinstein, G. (1998). *Family and intergenerational literacy in multilingual communities.* National Center for ESL Literacy Education (NCLE). Retrieved December 26, 2002, from May 3, 2006, http://www.cal.org/caela/esl_resources/digests/Famlit2.html

>Weinstein offers a good overview of family literacy from an adult education perspective.

Weinstein, G. (Ed.). (1999). *Learners' lives as curriculum: Six journeys to immigrant literacy.* Washington, DC: Delta Systems and the Center for Applied Linguistics.

>Weinstein discusses six successful family literacy projects in this collection.

Weinstein-Shr, G., & Quintero, E. (Eds.). (1995). *Immigrant learners and their families: Literacy to connect the generations.* McHenry, IL: Center for Applied Linguistics and Delta Systems.

>This collection of articles describes several family literacy programs developed for multilingual families.

Learner-centered Approach

English Skill Level: All
Grade Level: All
Also Called: Learner-Centered Curriculum

Background

The learner-centered approach is a general orientation toward language teaching that has evolved since the 1970s in reaction to teacher-fronted, top-down language teaching classrooms and curriculum. In general, a learner-centered approach focuses on the background, needs, and expectations of students to create a more effective, authentic, and focused language-learning environment. Information about students is obtained through various types of instruments used to determine students' needs and wants. From this information, curriculum and a syllabus are designed to help the students obtain their target goals. Activities in class also focus on activities in which students take an active role. As students' needs and abilities change, so may the curriculum and syllabus.

Strategy

1. An analysis is done to assess students' needs. Such an assessment may ask students what their goals are and what they are capable of doing now. A need analysis may also survey future professors or employers to see what they perceive to be the needs of future students or employees.

2. Curriculum, lessons, and activities are designed to help students reach the goals that they are targeting.

3. Curriculum, lessons, and activities may change throughout the length of the course as students' strengths, weaknesses, and goals are reevaluated.

4. At the end of the course, students may evaluate themselves or each other (or both). Ultimately the success of a learner-centered approach is based on whether students have the skills necessary to meet their target goals.

Strengths

- Instruction is based on student interests, needs, and background.
- Curriculum changes as needs change.

Weaknesses

- The ongoing assessment of student achievement needed to maximize effectiveness of this approach may frustrate teachers.

See also: Communicative Language Learning; Competency-based Approach; Critical Pedagogy; English for Specific Purposes

Further Reading

Brindley, G. (1989). *Assessing achievement in the learner-centered curriculum.* Sydney, Australia: National Centre for English Language Teaching and Research, Macquarie University.
    Brindley's discussion of criterion-referenced methods and techniques provides numerous examples, some of which come from practices of adult education ESL programs in Australia.

Ekbatani, G., & Pierso, H. (2000). *Learner-directed assessment in ESL.* Mahwah, NJ: Lawrence Erlbaum Associates.

This collection of essays discusses and demonstrates how to create assessment that focuses on the learner including several articles on self-assessment strategies.

Jacobsen, D. A., Eggen, P., & Kauchak, D. (1999). *Methods for teaching: Promoting student learning* (5th ed.). Upper Saddle River, NJ: Merrill/Prentice Hall.

This teacher-training textbook focuses on learner-centered planning, learner centered instruction, and learner-centered assessment.

Nunan. D. (1988). *The learner-centered curriculum: A study of second language teaching* (Cambridge Applied Linguistics series). Cambridge, England: Cambridge University Press.

Models of language instruction are synthesized within the context of a curriculum design.

Tudor, I. (1996). *Learner-centeredness as language education.* Cambridge, England: Cambridge University Press.

Tudor offers a holistic view of language learning in which students are viewed as the center of the classroom and teachers serve as facilitators of instruction.

Vocational English as a Second Language

English Skill Level: Advanced Beginning to Advanced
Grade Level: Secondary to Adult

Background

By and large, vocational English (VESL) grew out of adult education ESL programs that determined the need for programs that are more particularly focused on workplace skills. VESL developed to meet the needs of ESL students who planned on entering the workforce or who found employment and needed English skills to help them obtain other jobs or perform more effectively in their current positions. Some VESL programs focus on job-entry skills such as filling out job applications and interviewing. Other programs focus on skills needed in the workplace. Depending on the needs of the workplace, these programs may focus on clerical skills, computer skills, safety precautions, or the ability to communicate with coworkers.

Strategy

1. Decide where the program will take place (on or off the job site).

2. Determine, if not already known, who will pay for the program (e.g., the government, a private foundation, the place of work, or the student).

3. Complete a needs analysis of the students and the workplace. Which people need the training? What are their jobs? Will the students be paid for this training as part of their job, or will it be done outside of work?

4. Assess the English needs of the students and the company. Under what circumstances do students need to improve their English? What do the students feel they need to understand better? What do managers or other personnel feel isn't being understood?

5. Develop a curriculum and lessons to meet the needs of all concerned.

Strengths

- There is a focus on workplace skills. Students learn specific language and skills needed to enter the workforce or improve workplace communication.

- Classes can be offered at the workplace to accommodate students' schedules.

Weaknesses

- The language and skills are specific to the workplace and may not include other essential life skills.

- Employers or employees may not realize the difficulty of learning another language and thus have unreasonable expectations.

See also: Competency-based Approach; English for Specific Purposes

Further Reading

Buchanan, K. (1990). Vocational English as a second language programs. ERIC Clearinghouse on Languages and Linguistics Washington, DC. Retrieved May 3, 2006, http://www.nifl.gov/nifl-esl/2000/1333.html

Buchanan offers an overview of VESL programs.

Grognet, A. G. (1996). *Planning, implementing, and evaluating workplace ESL programs.* Retrieved May 3, 2006, from the Center for Adult English Acquisition Web site: http://www.cal.org/caela/esl_resources/digests/PLANNINGQA.html

The site offers a plethora of resources and additional information on a variety of instructional models and program for teaching adults learning English as a second language. Gognet's article supports the SCANS (Secretary's Commission on Achieving Necessary Skills) findings that advocate the integration of ESL and content instruction.

McGroarty, M., & Scott, S. (1993). *Workplace ESL instruction: Varieties and constraints.* Adjunct ERIC Clearinghouse for ESL Literacy Education, Washington DC. Retrieved from the National Clearinghouse for ESL Literacy Education Web site: http://www.ericdigests.org/1996-2/workplace.html

This document is a summary of programs that prepare non-English-speaking adults for the workplace.

Thomas, R. J., Gover, J., Cichon, D. J., Bird, L. A., & Harns, C. M. (1991). *Job-related language training for limited English proficient employees: A handbook for program developers.* Washington, DC: Development Assistance Corporation. Eric Document ED 342 277.

The authors advocate performing an extensive needs assessment that can inform the development of a job-related English language course for adults.

Bibliography

Articles and Books

Asher, J. (2000). *Learning another language through actions* (6th ed.). Los Gatos, CA: Sky Oaks Productions.

Auerbach, E. R. (2001). "Yes, but ...": Problematizing participatory ESL pedagogy. In P. Campbell & B. Burnaby (Eds.), *Participatory practices in adult education* (pp. 287–305). Mahwah, NJ: Lawrence Erlbaum Associates.

Auerbach, E. R. (1996). *Adult ESL/literacy from the community to the community: A guidebook for participatory literacy training*. Mahwah: NJ: Lawrence Erlbaum Associates.

Auerbach, E. R. (1992). *Making meaning, making change: Participatory curriculum development for adult ESL literacy*. Washington, DC: Center for Applied Linguistics.

Auerbach, E. (1989). Toward a socio-contextual approach to family literacy. *Harvard Educational Review, 59,* 165–181.

Auerbach, E. R. (1986). Competency-based ESL: One step forward or two steps back? *TESOL Quarterly, 20*(3), 411–429.

Barbier, S. (1994). *Troublesome English: A teaching grammar for ESOL instructors*. Englewood Cliffs, NJ: Prentice Hall Regents.

Barton, B. (Reteller). (1993). *The Little Red Hen big book*. New York: HarperTrophy.

Bernache, C. (1994). *Gateway to achievement in the content areas*. New York: McGraw-Hill/ Contemporary.

Blair, R. W. (1991). Innovative approaches. In M. Celce-Murcia (Ed.), *Teaching English as a second or foreign language* (2nd ed.). Boston: Heinle & Heinle.

Bowen, J. D., Madsen, H., & Hilferty, A. (1985). Where we've been: Insights from the past. In *TESOL: Techniques and procedures* (pp. 3–30). Boston: Heinle & Heinle.

Brindley, G. (1989). *Assessing achievement in the learner-centered curriculum*. Sydney, Australia: National Centre for English Language Teaching and Research, Macquarie University.

Brinton, D. (1997). *Insights: A content-based approach to academic preparation*. White Plains, NY: Longman.

Brinton, D. M., & Master, R. P. (Eds.). (1997). *New ways in content-based instruction*. Alexandra, VA: TESOL.

Brinton, D. M., Snow, M. A., & Wesche, M. B. (1989). *Content-based second language instruction*. Jakobovits, LA: Newbury House.

Brinton, D. M., Snow, M. A., & Wesche, M. D. (1993). Content-based second language instruction. In J. W. Oller (Ed.), *Methods that work: Ideas for literacy and language teachers* (2nd ed.). Boston: Heinle & Heinle.

Brown, D. H. (1998). *New vistas*. White Plains, NY: Longman.

Brown, H. D. (1994). *Teaching by principles: An interactive approach to language pedagogy*. Upper Saddle, NJ: Prentice Hall.

Brumfit, C. J., & Johnson, K. (Eds.). (1979). *The communicative approach to language teaching.* Oxford, England: Oxford University Press.

Buchanan, K. (1990). Vocational English as a second language programs. Retrieved from the ERIC Clearinghouse on Languages and Linguistics Web site: http://www.nifl.gov/nifl-esl/ 2000/1333.html

Burton, E. (1995). *Going places: Picture-based English.* White Plains, NY: Longman.

Bygate, M., Skehan, P., & Swain, M. (Eds.). (2001). *Researching pedagogic tasks: Second language learning, teaching and testing.* Harlow, England: Longman.

Canale, M., & Swain, M. (1980). Theoretical bases of communicative approaches to second language teaching. *Applied Linguistics, I*(1), 1–47.

Carver, T. K., & Fotinos, S. D. (1997). *A conversation book* (books 1 and 2). White Plains, NY: Longman.

Chamot, A. U. (1999). *America: The early years (up to the 1800's).* White Plains, NY: Longman.

Chamot, A. U. (1999) *America: After Independence (1800–1900).* White Plains, NY: Longman.

Chamot, A. U., et al. (2000). *Perspectives 2000* (books 1 and 2). Boston: Heinle & Heinle.

Chamot, A. U., & O'Malley, J. M. (1994). *The CALLA handbook: Implementing the cognitive academic language learning approach.* Reading, MA: Addison-Wesley.

Chamot, A. U., & O'Malley, J. M. (1994). Part three: Implementing CALLA in the classroom. In *The CALLA handbook: Implementing the cognitive academic language learning approach* (pp. 191–320). Reading, MA: Addison-Wesley.

Chamot, A. U., & O'Malley, J. M. (1992). The cognitive academic language learning approach: A bridge to the mainstream. In P. A. Richard-Amato & M. A. Snow (Eds.), *The multicultural classroom: Readings for content-area teachers.* Reading, MA: Addison-Wesley.

Chamot, A. U., O'Malley, J. M., & Kupper, L. (1992). *Building bridges: Content and learning strategies for ESL* (books 1–3). Boston: Heinle & Heinle.

Chastain, K. (1971). *The development of modern language skills: Theory to practice.* Philadelphia: Center for Curriculum Development.

Christison, M. A., & Bassano, S. (1997). *Earth and physical science: Content and learning strategies.* Reading, MA: Longman.

Christison, M. A., & Bassano, S. (1997). *Life science: Content and learning strategies.* Reading, MA: Longman.

Christison, M. A., & Bassano, S. (1997). *Social studies: Content and learning strategies.* Reading, MA: Longman.

Celce-Murcia, M. (2001). Language teaching approaches: An overview. In *Teaching English as a second or foreign language* (3rd ed., pp. 1–11). Boston: Heinle & Heinle.

Celce-Murcia, M. (1991). Grammar pedagogy in second and foreign language teaching. *TESOL Quarterly, 25,* 3.

Colvin, R. J. (1986). *I speak English: A tutor's guide to teaching conversational English* (3rd ed.). Syracuse, NY: Literacy Volunteers of America.

Connerton, P., & Reid, F. (1997). *Linkages: A content-based integrated skills program.* Boston: Heinle & Heinle.

Crandall, J. (Ed.). (1995). *ESL through content-area instruction: Mathematics, science, social studies* (Language Education: Theory and Practice 67). McHenry, IL: Center for Applied Linguistics.

DeCarrico, J. S. (2001). Vocabulary learning and teaching. In M. Celce-Murcia (Ed.), *Teaching English as a second or foreign language* (3rd ed., pp. 285–299). Boston: Heinle & Heinle.

DeFilippo, J., & Skidmore, C. (2004). *Skill sharpener* (2nd ed.). White Plains, NY: Longman.

Douglas, D. (2000). *Assessing languages for specific purposes.* Cambridge, England: Cambridge University Press.

Dudley-Evans, T. (2001). English for specific purposes. In R. Carter & D. Nunan (Eds.), *The Cambridge guide to teaching English to speakers of other languages* (pp. 131–136). Cambridge, England: Cambridge University Press.

Dudley-Evans, T., & St. John, M. J. (1998). *Developments in ESP: A multi-disciplinary approach.* Cambridge, England: Cambridge University Press

Enright, D. S. (1991). *Teaching English as a second or foreign language.* Boston: Heinle & Heinle.

Ekbatani, G., & Pierso, H. (2000). *Learner-directed assessment in ESL.* Mahwah, NJ: Lawrence Erlbaum Associates.

Espeseth, M. (1996). *Academic listening encounters: Listening, note taking, and discussion, content focus: Human behavior.* New York: Cambridge University Press.

Eyring, J. L. (2001). Experiential and negotiated language learning. In M. Celce-Murcia (Ed.), *Teaching English as a second or foreign language* (pp. 333–344). Boston: Heinle & Heinle.

Ferris, D., & Tagg, T. (1996). Academic listening/speaking tasks for ESL students: Problems, suggestions, and implications. *TESOL Quarterly, 30*(2), 297–317.

Fidere, A. (1999). *Practical assessments for literature-based reading classrooms.* New York: Scholastic.

Finocchiaro, M., & Brumfit, C. (1983). *The functional-notational approach.* New York: Oxford University Press.

Fitzsimmons, P. (2002). *Kick starting the inner site: Reading to see and feel.* Brisbane, Australia: Annual Meeting for the Australian Association for Research in Education. ERIC Document Reproduction Service No. ED478114

Flowerdew, J., & Peacock, M. (2001). *Research perspectives on English for academic purposes.* Cambridge, England: Cambridge University Press

Foley, B. H., & Neblett, E. R. (2003). *The new grammar in action: An integrated course in English.* Boston: Heinle & Heinle.

Fox, G. (1998). Using corpus data in the classroom. In B. Tomlinson (Ed.), *Materials development in language teaching* (pp. 25–43). Cambridge, England: Cambridge University Press.

Freeman, Y. S., & Freeman, D. E. (1998). *ESL/EFL teaching: Principles for success.* Portsmouth, NH: Heinemann.

Froese, V. (Ed.). (1996). *Whole language practice and theory* (2nd ed.). Boston: Allyn & Bacon.

Grabe, W., & Stoller, F. L. (2001). *Teaching English as a second or foreign language* (3rd ed.). Boston: Heinle & Heinle.

Grognet, A. G. (1996). *Planning, implementing, and evaluating workplace ESL programs.* Retrieved May 3, 2006, from the Center for Adult English Acquisition Web site: http://www.cal.org/caela/esl_resources/digests/PLANNINGQA.html

Gomez, S., et al. (1995). *Eureka: Science demonstrations for ESL classes.* Reading, MA: Addison-Wesley.

Harp, B. (Ed.). (1991). *Assessment and evaluation in whole language programs.* Norwood, MA: Christopher-Gordon.

Harris, T. (1995). *Exploring English. A. Rowe, Illustrator.* White Plains, NY: Longman.

Hawkins, B. (1991). Teaching children to read in a second language. In M. Celce-Murcia (Ed.), *Teaching English as a second or foreign language.* Boston: Heinle & Heinle.

Holme, R. (1996). *ESP ideas: Recipes for teaching academic and professional English.* Canterbury, England: Pilgrims/Longman UK.

Holt, D. H., & Van Duzer, C. H. (Eds.). (2000). *Assessing success in family literacy and adult ESL.* Washington, DC: Center for Applied Linguistics and Delta Systems.

Hones, D. F. (1999). US Justice? Critical pedagogy and the case of Mumia Abu-Jamal. *TESOL Journal, 8*(4), 27–33.

Hutchinson, T., & Waters, A. (1987). *English for specific purposes: A learning-centred approach.* Cambridge, England: Cambridge University Press.

Hurley, S. R., & Tinajero, V. J. (2001). *Literacy assessment of second language learners.* Boston: Allyn & Bacon.

Iwamoto, J. R. (1994). *Coming together, book 1: Integrating math and language in a sheltered approach to mathematics for secondary students.* White Plains, NY: Longman.

Iwamoto, J. R. (1994). *Coming together, book 2: Integrating math and language in a sheltered approach to mathematics for secondary students.* White Plains, NY: Longman.

Jacobsen, D. A., Eggen, P., & Kauchak, D. (1999). *Methods for teaching: Promoting student learning* (5th ed.). Upper Saddle River, NJ: Merrill/Prentice Hall.

Jenkins, R., & Sabbagh, S. L. (2001). *Stand out: Standards-based English,* books 1–4. Boston: Heinle & Heinle.

Johns, A. M., & Price-Machado, D. (2001). English for specific purposes: Tailoring courses to student needs—and to the outside world. In M. Celce-Murcia (Ed.), *Teaching English as a second or foreign language* (3rd ed., pp. 43–54). Boston: Heinle and Heinle.

Johnson, D.M. (1994). *Educating second language children: The whole child, the whole curriculum, the whole community.* Cambridge, England: Cambridge University Press.

Jordan, R. (1997). *English for academic purposes: A guide and resource book for teachers.* Cambridge, England: Cambridge University Press.

Kasper, L. F. (Ed.). (2000). *Content-based college ESL instruction.* Mahwah, NJ: Lawrence Erlbaum Associates.

Kauffman, D., & Apple, G. (2000). *The Oxford picture dictionary for the content areas.* Oxford University Press.

Kerwin, M. (1995). *Topics and language competencies.* White Plains, NY: Prentice Hall.

Kessler, C. (1992). *Cooperative language learning: A teacher's resource book.* Englewood Cliffs, NJ: Prentice Hall.

Krashen, S. (1995). What is intermediate natural approach? In P. Hashinpur, R. Maldonado, & M. VanNaerson (Eds.), *Studies in language learning and Spanish linguistics in honor of Tracy D. Terrell* (pp. 92–105). New York: McGraw-Hill.

Krashen, S. D. (1993). Sheltered subject-matter teaching. In J. W. Oller (Ed.), *Methods that work: Ideas for literacy and language teachers* (2nd ed.). Boston: Heinle & Heinle.

Krashen, S., & Terrell, T. (1983). *The natural approach: Language acquisition in the classroom.* Englewood Cliffs, NJ: Prentice Hall.

Larimer, R. E., & Schleicher, L. (Eds.). (1999). *New ways in using authentic materials in the classroom.* Alexandra, VA: TESOL.

Larsen-Freeman, D. (1997). *Grammar and its teaching: Challenging the myths.* Washington, DC: Eric Clearinghouse on Language and Literature Retrieved May 3, 2006, http://www.cal.org/resources/digest/larsen01.html

Larsen-Freeman, D. (2000). Community language learning. In *Techniques and principles in language teaching* (2nd ed., pp. 89–106). Oxford, England: Oxford University Press.

Larsen-Freeman, D. (2000). The audio-lingual method. In *Principles and techniques of language teaching* (2nd ed., pp. 35–51). Oxford, England: Oxford University Press.

Larsen-Freeman, D. (2000). *Techniques and principles in language teaching* (2nd ed.). Oxford, England: Oxford University Press.

Lee, J. F., & VanPatten, B. (1995). *Making communicative language teaching happen.* New York: McGraw-Hill.

Lewis, M. (Ed.). (2000). *Teaching collocation: Further developments in the lexical approach.* Hove, England: Language Teaching Publications.

Lewis, M. (1997). *Implementing the lexical approach: Putting theory into practice.* Hove, England: Language Teaching Publications.

Lock, G. (1996). *Functional English grammar: An introduction for second language learners.* Cambridge, England: Cambridge University Press.

Lubawy, S. (2000). *World view: A global study of geography, history, and culture.* Palatine, IL: Linmore.

Magy, R. (1998). *Working it out: Interactive English for the workplace.* Boston: Heinle & Heinle.

Marsh, V. (2000). *Total physical response storytelling: A communicative approach to language learning.* Retrieved April 28, 2006, from http://www.tprstorytelling.com/story.htm

Master, P., & Brinton, D. (Eds.). (1998). *New ways in English for specific purposes.* Alexandria, VA: TESOL.

McGarry, R. G. (1998). Professional writing for business administration: An adjunct, content-based course. *TESOL Journal, 7*(6), 28–31.

Molinsky, S. J., & Bliss, B. (1995). *Expressways.* White Plains, NY: Longman.

Molinsky, S. J., & Bliss, B. (2000). *Side by side* (3rd ed.). White Plains, NY: Longman.

Morgan, B. D. (1998). *The ESL classroom: Teaching, critical practice, and community development.* Toronto: University of Toronto Press.

Morrow, L. M. (Ed.). (1995). *Family literacy: Connections in schools and communities.* New Brunswick, NJ: Rutgers University.

Morrow, L. M., Tracey, D. H., & Maxwell, C. M. (Eds.). (1995). *A survey of family literacy in the United States.* Newark, DE: International Reading Association.

Moss, D., & Van Duzer, C. (1998). *Project-based learning for adult English language learners.* National Center for ESL Literacy Education. Retrieved November 17, 2005, from http://www.eric.ed.gov/ (ERIC # ED427556)

Nation, P. (Ed.). (1995). *New ways in teaching vocabulary.* Alexandra, VA: Teachers of English to Students of Other Languages (TESOL).

Nattinger, J. R., & DeCarrico, J. S. (1992) *Lexical phrases and language teaching.* Oxford, England: Oxford University Press.

Nelson, V. (1999). *Building skills for social studies: Reading skills, writing skills, communication skills, math skills, map skills, charting & graphing skills, science skills, timeline skills.* New York: McGraw-Hill/Contemporary.

Nelson, G., & Winters, T. (1993). *Operations in English: 55 natural and logical sequences for language acquisition.* Brattleboro, VT: Pro Lingua Associates.

Nunan, D. (2001). *Expressions: Meaningful English communication.* Boston: Heinle & Heinle.

Nunan, D. (1992). *Collaborative language learning and teaching.* Cambridge, England: Cambridge University Press.

Nunan, D. (1989). *Designing tasks for the communicative classroom.* Cambridge, England: Cambridge University Press.

Nunan, D. (1988). *The learner-centered curriculum: A study of second language teaching* (Cambridge Applied Linguistics series). Cambridge, England: Cambridge University Press.

Pally, M. (2000). *Sustained content teaching in academic ESL/EFL.* Boston: Houghton-Mifflin.

Pally, M., & Bailey, N. (Eds.). (1999). *Sustained content teaching in academic ESL/EFL: A practical approach.* Boston: Houghton-Mifflin.

Pomann, H., & Foley, B. H. (1982). *Lifelines: Coping skills in English.* White Plains, NY: Longman.

Pennington, M. C. (Ed.). (1995). *New ways in teaching grammar.* Alexandra, VA: Teachers of Students of Other Languages (TESOL).

Peyton, J., & Crandall, J. (1995). *Philosophies and approaches in adult ESL literacy instruction.* Retrieved May 3, 2006, from http://www.ericdigest.org/1996-2/esl.html

Prapphal, K. (1993). *Methods that work: Ideas for literacy and language teachers* (2nd ed.). Boston: Heinle & Heinle.

Price-Machado, D. (1998). *Skills for success: Working and studying in English.* New York: Cambridge University Press.

Richards, J. C., & Rodgers, T. S. (2001). The audiolingual method. In *Approaches and methods in language teaching: A description and analysis* (pp. 50–69). Cambridge, England: Cambridge University Press.

Richards, J. C., & Rodgers, T. S. (2001). Community language learning. In *Approaches and methods in language teaching* (2nd ed., pp. 90–99). Cambridge, England: Cambridge University Press.

Richards, J. C., & Rodgers, T. S. (2001). *Competency-based language teaching in approaches and methods in language teaching* (2nd ed., pp. 141–150). Cambridge, England: Cambridge University Press.

Richards, J. C., & Rodgers, T. S. (2001). The silent way. In *Approaches and methods in language teaching* (2nd ed., pp. 81–89). Cambridge, England: Cambridge University Press.

Richards, J. C., & Rodgers, T. S. (2001). Suggestopedia. In *Approaches and methods in language learning* (2nd ed., pp. 100–107). Cambridge, England: Cambridge University Press.

Richard-Amato, P. A. (1996). *Making it happen: Interaction in the second language classroom—from theory to practice.* New York: Longman.

Richard-Amato, P. A. (1996). The natural approach: How it is evolving. In P. A. Richard-Amato *Making it happen: Interaction in the second language classroom* (pp. 127–154). White Plains, NY: Addison-Wesley.

Richard-Amato, P. A. (1996). The total physical response and the audio-motor unit. In *Making it happen: Interaction in the second language classroom* (pp. 115–126). White Plains, NY: Longman.

Richard-Amato, P. A., & Snow, M. A. (1996). A secondary sheltered English model. In *Making it happen: Interaction in the second language classroom* (pp. 334–338). Reading, MA: Addison-Wesley.

Rivers, W. (1987). *Interactive language teaching.* Cambridge, England: Cambridge University Press.

Rodrigues, R. J., & White, R. H. (1993). From role play to the real world. In J. W. Oller (Ed.), *Methods that work: Ideas for literacy and language teachers* (2nd ed.). Boston: Heinle & Heinle.

Raines, S. C. (Ed.). (1995). *Whole language across the curriculum: Grades 1, 2, and 3.* New York: Teachers College Press and Newark, DE: The International Reading Association.

Sagliano, M., & Greenfield, K. (1998). A collaborative model of content-based EFL instruction in the liberal arts. *TESOL Journal, 7*(3), 23–28.

Saslow, J., & Collins, T. (2001). *Workplace plus.* White Plains, NY: Longman.

Savignon, S. J. (1983). *Communicative competence: Theory and classroom practice.* Reading, MA: Addison-Wesley.

Savignon, S. J. (1997). *Communicative competence: Theory and classroom practice* (2nd ed.). New York: McGraw-Hill.

Savignon, S. J. (2001). Communicative language teaching for the twenty-first century. In M. Celce-Murcia (Ed.), *Teaching English as a second or foreign language* (3rd ed., pp. 13–28). Boston: Heinle & Heinle.

Scarcella, R. C., Anderson, E. S., & Krashen, S. (Eds.). (1990). *Developing competence in a second language.* New York: Harper & Row.

Scarcella, R. C., & Oxford, R. L. (1992). *The tapestry of language learning; the individual in the communicative classroom.* Boston. Heinle & Heinle.

Schmitt, N., & Carter, R. (2000) The lexical advantages of narrow reading for second language learners. *TESOL Journal, 9*(1) 4–9.

Seal, B. (1996). *Academic encounters: Reading, study skills, and writing, content focus: Human behavior.* Cambridge, England: Cambridge University Press.

Seely, C., & Romijn, E. K. (1995). *TPR is more than commands—at all levels.* Los Gatos, CA: Sky Oaks Production.

Shameem, N., & Tickoo, M. (Eds.). (1999). *New ways in using communicative games in language teaching.* Alexandra, VA: TESOL.

Shore, I. (1987). *Friere for the classroom.* Portsmouth, NH: Heineman.

Snow, M. A. (2001). Content-based and immersion models for second and foreign language teaching. In Celce-Murcia (Ed.), *Teaching English as a second or foreign language* (3rd ed., pp. 303–318). Boston: Heinle & Heinle.

Snow, M. A., & Brinton, D. M. (Eds.). (1997). *Content-based classroom: Perspectives on integrating language and content.* White Plains, NY: Longman.

Stevick, E. W. (1998). *Working with teaching methods: What's at stake?* Boston: Heinle & Heinle.

Stevick, E. (1980). The work of Georgi Lozanov. In *Teaching language: A way and ways* (pp. 229–243). Boston: Heinle & Heinle.

Stevick, E. (1980). Some suggestopedic ideas in non-suggestopedic methods. In *Teaching language: A way and ways* (pp. 244–259). Boston: Heinle & Heinle.

Stevick, E. (1980). One way of teaching: The silent way. In *Teaching languages: A way and ways* (pp. 37–84). Boston: Heinle & Heinle.

Taylor, D. (Ed.). (1997). *Many families, many literacies: An international declaration of principles.* Portsmouth, NH: Heinemann.

Taylor, M. T. (1993). *The language experience approach and adult learners.* National Center for ESL Literacy Education. Retrieved May 4, 2006, from http://www.cal.org/caela/esl_resources/digests/LEA.html

Terdy, D. (1986). *Content area ESL: Social studies.* Palatine, IL: Linmore.

Terrell, T. (1991). The role of grammar instruction in a communicative approach. *The Modern Language Journal, 75*(1), 52–63.

TESOL Journal. (1999, summer). *Collaborative classrooms: Where competence, confidence, and creativity converge, 8*(2).

TESOL Quarterly. (1999). *TESOL Quarterly 33*(3).

Tudor, I. (1996). *Learner-centeredness as language education.* Cambridge, England: Cambridge University Press.

Van Duzer, C., & Cunningham Florez, M. A. (1999). *Critical literacy for adult English language learners.* Washington, DC: National Clearinghouse for ESL Literacy Education (EDO-LE-99-07). Retrieved May 4, 2006, from http://www.cal.org/caela/esl_resources/digests/Famlit2.html

U.S. Department of Labor. (1993). *Teaching the SCANS competencies.* ERIC Document ED 354 400.

Weinstein, G. (Ed.). (1999). *Learners' lives as curriculum: Six journeys to immigrant literacy.* Washington, DC: Delta Systems and the Center for Applied Linguistics.

Weinstein, G. (1998). *Family and intergenerational literacy in multilingual communities.* National Center for ESL Literacy Education (NCLE). Retrieved December 26, 2002, from http://www.cal.org/ncle/DIGESTS/FamLit2.HTM

Weinstein-Shr, G., et al. (1996). *Collaborations: English in our lives, a 5-level series.* Boston: Heinle & Heinle.

Weinstein-Shr, G., & Quintero, E. (Eds.). (1995). *Immigrant learners and their families: Literacy to connect the generations.* McHenry, IL: Center for Applied Linguistics and Delta Systems.

Whetzel, D. (1992). *The Secretary of Labor's Commission on Achieving Necessary Skills.* ERIC Document ED339749.

Whitmore, K. F., & Crowell, C. G. (1994). *Inventing a classroom: Life in a bilingual, whole language learning community.* York, ME: Stenhouse Publishers.

Wichman, A., Fligelstone, S., McEnery, T., & Knowles, G. (Eds.). (1997). *Teaching and language corpora.* London: Longman.

Wilberg, P. (1987*). One to one: A teacher's handbook.* Hove, England: Language Teaching Publications.

Willis, D., & Willis, J. (2001). Task-based language learning. In R. Carter & D. Nunan (Eds.), *The Cambridge guide to teaching English to speakers of other languages* (pp. 173–179). Cambridge, English: Cambridge University Press.

Willis, J. (1998). Concordances in the classroom without a computer: Assembling and exploiting concordances of common words. In B. Tomlinson (Ed.), *Materials development in language teaching* (pp. 44–66.) Cambridge, England: Cambridge University Press.

Willis, J. (1996). *A framework for task-based learning.* Essex, England: Addison Wesley Longman.

Wink, J. (1997). *Critical pedagogy: Notes from the real world.* Los Angeles: California Association of Bilingual Education.

Wolfe, P. M. (1996). Literacy bargains: Toward a critical literacy in a multilingual classroom. *TESOL Journal, 5(4),* 22–26.

Zimmerman, F. (1989). *English for science.* White Plains, NY: Longman.

Computer Assisted Language Learning (CALL)

Grammar approaches lend themselves well to computer programs. A number of recent ESL grammar textbooks now have accompanying CDs and Web sites. Other grammar-practice software include the following:

English on call, McGraw-Hill Contemporary

ESL fitness, Merit Software

ESL picture grammar, available from Audio-Forum

Focus on grammar CD-ROM, Longman

Grammar 3D: Contextualized practice for learners of English, Heinle & Heinle

The grammar cracker, Miller Educational Materials

Let's go, Miller Educational Materials

Rosetta stone, Fairfield Technologies.

Verbcon, Audio-Forum

Index

About the Authors

DEBORAH L. NORLAND, Ph.D. is a professor of education at Luther College. She supervises ELL teachers and teaches TESOL methods classes and directs a summer reading program for ELL children on the Navajo reservation.

TERRY PRUETT-SAID is a former ESL instructor of adults and children and is currently an ESL adjunct professor at Macomb Community College.

Lightning Source UK Ltd.
Milton Keynes UK
UKOW02f1917230214

226994UK00009B/53/P